SUNLIGHT SPEECH
That DISPELS *the*
DARKNESS *of* DOUBT

BOOKS BY THINLEY NORBU

A Brief Fantasy History of a Himalayan

A Cascading Waterfall of Nectar

Magic Dance: The Display of the Self-Nature of the
Five Wisdom Dakinis

The Small Golden Key to the Treasure of the Various Essential
Necessities of General and Extraordinary Buddhist Dharma

The Sole Panacea: A Brief Commentary on the Seven-Line Prayer to
Guru Rinpoche That Cures the Suffering of the Sickness of Karma
and Defilement

Sunlight Speech That Dispels the Darkness of Doubt:
Sublime Prayers, Praises, and Practices of the Nyingma Masters

Welcoming Flowers from Across the Cleansed Threshold of Hope:
An Answer to the Pope's Criticism of Buddhism

White Sail: Crossing the Waves of Ocean Mind to the Serene
Continent of the Triple Gems

SUNLIGHT SPEECH
That DISPELS *the*
DARKNESS *of* DOUBT

Sublime Prayers, Praises, and Practices
of the Nyingma Masters

Compiled and translated by THINLEY NORBU

Written by the Omniscient Emanations of Buddha

KUNKHYEN LONGCHENPA

RIGDZIN JIGME LINGPA

PATRUL RINPOCHE

MIPHAM RINPOCHE

KYABJE DUDJOM RINPOCHE

Shambhala
BOSTON & LONDON
2015

Shambhala Publications, Inc.
Horticultural Hall
300 Massachusetts Avenue
Boston, Massachusetts 02115
www.shambhala.com

9 8 7 6 5 4 3 2 1

First Edition
Printed in the United States of America

♾ This edition is printed on acid-free paper that meets
the American National Standards Institute Z39.48 Standard.
♻ This book is printed on 30% postconsumer recycled paper.
For more information please visit www.shambhala.com.

Distributed in the United States by Penguin Random House LLC
and in Canada by Random House of Canada Ltd

Designed by Michael Russem

LIBRARY OF CONGRESS CATALOGING-IN-PUBLICATION DATA

Sunlight speech that dispels the darkness of doubt: sublime prayers, praises,
and practices of the Nyingma masters / by the omniscient emanations of
Buddha, Kunkhyen Longchenpa, Rigdzin Jigme Lingpa, Mipham Rinpoche,
Paltrul Rinpoche, Khyabje Düdjom Rinpoche; Translated by Thinley
Norbu.—First edition.
pages   cm
Includes bibliographical references.
Includes translations from Tibetan.
ISBN 978-1-57062-244-1 (hardcover: alk. paper) 1. Rñiṅ-ma-pa (Sect)—
Doctrines. I. Klon-chen-pa Dri-med-'od-zer, 1308–1363. II. Thinley Norbu,
translator.
BQ7662.4.S86 2014
294.3'420423—dc23
2014007265

Contents

TEACHINGS AND SADHANAS

Note to the Reader

The portraits of Kunkhyen Longchenpa (left) and Rigdzin Jigme Lingpa Rinpoche (right) that appear following page 50 are reproductions of two small, cherished personal thangkas belonging to Kyabje Thinley Norbu Rinpoche, who took them everywhere in an altar suitcase, even on flights. They were painted by a thangka artist in Bhutan who was known for having a special gift, or *kabap* (*bka' babs*), for painting these two sublime beings, and they are considered to be actual likenesses of these masters from centuries past.

Italics have been employed in a special way in this book (in addition to their usual use for titles of works). They are used in sadhanas to distinguish instructions and commentary from the text to be recited. For example:

Chapter 6, "The Treasure of Blessings of the Ritual of Buddha," contains italicized portions that are mainly instructions by Mipham Rinpoche, the author of the puja, except for one interpolation in brackets ("Also by Mipham Rinpoche," added by Kyabje Thinley Norbu Rinpoche).

Chapter 7, "The Sadhana of Fully Enlightened Supreme Vajrasattva, Called 'The Daily Practice of the Profound Path, Contained in Essence,'" contains italicized instructions, which are not to be recited by the practitioner.

Chapter 8, "The Rain of Blessings: Guru Yoga in Connection with the Seven-Line Prayer," contains italicized portions that are instructions and commentary by the author, Mipham Rinpoche.

Chapter 11, "The Guru Yoga of Receiving Wish-Fulfilling Great Flawless Exaltation," contains italicized portions that are instructions and commentary by the author, Kyabje Dudjom Rinpoche.

Introduction

Until the occupation of Tibet by the communist Chinese, there were many great sublime saints in that land among the lineage holders of the Nyingma tradition of Buddhism. Some of the most precious of these saints were Gyalwa Longchen Rabjam, Kunkhyen Jigme Lingpa, Patrul Rinpoche, Mipham Rinpoche, and Kyabje Dudjom Rinpoche, whose writings are contained in this book.

Originally, Sandra Scales requested that I translate *Mindfulness, the Ocean of Qualities* by Rigdzin Jigme Lingpa, and this was done with her assistance. Also included in this book are *The Practice of the View, Meditation, and Action, Called "The Sublime Heart Jewel"* by Patrul Rinpoche; a revision of a translation I did many years ago of *The Lion's Roar* by Rigdzin Jigme Lingpa; and *Always Rejoicing in the Forest*, by Kunkhyen Longchenpa. This book also contains translations of several prayers and sadhanas, including *Praise of the Ten Deeds of Buddha* by Rigdzin Jigme Lingpa; *The Treasure of Blessings of the Ritual of Buddha* and *The Rain of Blessings: Guru Yoga in Connection with the Seven-Line Prayer* by Mipham Rinpoche; and *The Sadhana of Fully Enlightened Supreme Vajrasattva, Called "The Daily Practice of the Profound Path, Contained in Essence"; The Assembly Palace of Great Flawless Exaltation, Radiant Lotus Light; Calling the Lama;* and *The Guru Yoga of Receiving Wish-Fulfilling Great Flawless Exaltation* by Kyabje Dudjom Rinpoche.

In general, when translating any Buddhist teachings from Tibetan into English, especially precious wisdom teachings, there is a language problem, since it is difficult to connect substantial, nihilist, ordinary expressions with insubstantial wisdom expressions. Dharma words are connected to mind, mind is connected to wisdom, and wisdom is intangible. Therefore, whoever translates Dharma must try predominantly to write about the intangible qualities of wisdom. So it is awkward and not such a good idea to translate these teachings into English, since English is predominantly a materialistic language that does not have suitable words for the profound, intangible appearance of qualities completely revealed by Tibetan terms. If words are chosen with the misinterpretation of substantial word habit, these qualities can be turned into ordinary intellectual, philosophical, or material conceptions. For those who like to study or practice Buddhism, it is of great benefit to learn literary Tibetan rather than reading translations, since it is the most vast and profound language in the world in this generation for conveying pure spiritual meaning.

If these precious teachings are not printed, then it is difficult for them to be perpetuated and they may be lost. If they are printed, then they may be misused and lost to nonpractitioners who do not have faith. Especially in this degenerate age, even though many people seem to be interested in Buddhist ideas, they actually consider what they learn to be cultural phenomena that they are excited to fit within their own conceptions. This is impossible, since the vast Buddhist view is beyond the imaginings of tangible samsaric phenomena.

The precious teachings of Buddhism should be the cause of faith, practice, and enlightenment. Even if I do not translate them, many of these teachings have been translated, are being translated, and will be translated. Also, according to the Mahayana, all beings, including humans, have the root circumstance of Buddha nature, which can blossom through the contributing circumstance of precious sublime teachings for those with gifted, keen faculties, pure faith, and the intention to practice. So I translated these teachings in a simple way, trying not to create sophisticated ideas, giving some of the words as they are in Tibetan since they have their own power.

I hope that whoever reads this book will do so with faith and the prayer to make a connection with the teachings it contains so that Buddha nature will blossom. In order to respect these teachings and for the accumulation of virtue, keep this and all precious Buddhist books safely on an altar or in a high place as an image of Buddha's sublime speech, according to Buddha's instruction, and as an affirmation of the Dharma vows of taking refuge in the Triple Gems. We may think that Buddha has no conception of lower or higher, Dharma has no contradiction between impure and pure, and books have no judgment about what is wrong or right; but we have conceptions, contradictions, and judgments from the dualistic habit of many lives until attaining nondualistic pure wisdom phenomena. It is the responsibility of the reader not to just treat this book like an ordinary newspaper, reading it once and then throwing it on the floor and stepping on it. We should recognize that it is not just paper and ink, but blesses our minds to open toward enlightenment. Read it with faith, increasing mind's qualities. It is the same as Buddha's speech.

Through this virtue, may all sentient beings, including sponsors who have given their support and help, reach enlightenment.

KYABJE THINLEY NORBU RINPOCHE

PRAISES

Praise to Longchenpa

Like the Six Ornaments and Two Excellences[1] who beautify
    the world,
You hold the power of compassion, the revealed meaning
    of Buddha's speech, and the realization of nondualistic
    wisdom appearance.
Yet even so, your sublime activity is hidden in a forest of
    holy solitude.[2]
Great Profound One who completely perfected samsara and
    enlightenment in the state of Dharmakaya, Stainless
    Rays of Light, I pray at your feet.

Praise to Jigme Lingpa

Knowing all of whatever exists to be known, treasure of
     compassion for sentient beings,
Re-emanation of Stainless Rays of Light, and treasury of
     wisdom mind revelations,
Great profound expanse of light, sky-mind yogi,
Fearless Sublime Islander,[3] I pray at your feet.

Praise to Manjushri

MIPHAM RINPOCHE

OM SWASTI

Changeless auspiciousness of the Triple Gems,
The source from which manifesting occurs,
The supreme refuge of refuges,
Holder of the excellent Glory of Perfected Glory,

Even though you magically dance before sentient beings
In complement to their phenomena of direction and time,
If whatever is known is examined,
You never remain anywhere: I prostrate to you.
The most peaceful in peace,
Excellent flawless Perfected Glory,
Sky-pervading body of great compassion
In the display of youthfulness, I prostrate to you.

The most wrathful in wrath,
Destroyer of the Lord of Death, annihilating all death
        phenomena,
Devouring samsara and nirvana in the mouth of stainless
        space,
Great enemy of time, I prostrate to you.

Indestructible body of inseparable appearance and
    emptiness,
Absolute wisdom victor of all without anything remaining,
Holder of the expanse of Kuntuzangpo,
Indestructible Perfected Glory, I prostrate to you.

Prostrating and praising you,
By this virtue, until attaining enlightenment,
Glory of Perfected Glory,
May the light of wisdom be absorbed into the lotus heart.

Praise to the Melodious Wisdom Goddess Saraswati, Called "The Melody of the Youthful Display of Joy"

KUNKHYEN LONGCHENPA

I prostrate to the deity of poetry.

Wisdom goddess of the supreme nature of ecstasy,
Staying in the great continent of the ocean of qualities,
Mother of all Buddhas and Bodhisattvas,
I prostrate to Saraswati.

From the melting snow-mountain of compassion,
The wisdom goddess is freshly born
And a river of poetry slowly flows.
I prostrate to Saraswati.

As beautiful as the full moon on the fifteenth day,
With the smiling face of a sixteen-year-old,
Adorned with lightly ringing rosary ornaments,
To Saraswati, I prostrate.

Like a lotus, sitting on a lotus and moon,
Like an extremely white magnificent snow mountain,

Like gathering white clouds of autumn,
To Saraswati, I prostrate.

With the white face of a moon glowing with light,
Sitting on the throne of a full moon,
With a backrest of a moon,
To Saraswati, I prostrate.

The strength of an elephant, the radiance of the moon,
And the complexion of a lake-born flower[4] are overpowered
By your continuous sun-like beauty.
I prostrate to Saraswati.

If this snow mountain had lotus eyes,
It would resemble your gleaming face.
You are like the peak of a snow mountain.
I prostrate to Saraswati.

Again and again, I remember your body
And immerse my mind in the sounds A and AH,
Dispelling darkness by the practice of HRING HRING.
I prostrate to Saraswati.

O beautiful yogini heroine,
Today, you are like a rainbow in the sky,
Like a reflection of appearance and non-appearance.
I prostrate to Saraswati.

In the form of your body of light,
White, yellow, red, and green

Distinct and combined lights brilliantly radiate.
I prostrate to Saraswati.

For some, in a canopy of clouds,
Your clear form in white, red, and blue
Appears as a playful, supreme, and tranquil body.
I prostrate to Saraswati.

For some, in the light of the sun, lotus, and moon,
In the form of the five lights radiating light,
You are waving fans and playing the lute and flute.
I prostrate to Saraswati.

For some, in light and stars,
Instantly, instantly you are emanating,
Illuminating miracles of appearance and non-appearance.
I prostrate to Saraswati.

For some you are manifesting
And completely manifested in a halo of light,
Smiling beautifully with various radiant lights.
I prostrate to Saraswati.

Ah, fortunate, noble wisdom goddess,
What was wished for, for so long, is accomplished today.
Again, whenever I wish to see you, hear you, and ask about you,
Please, at that moment, may your wisdom body appear.

May you keep all who have faith
In you and all your sons

With the moon of the supreme whiteness
Of your expansive, omniscient wisdom mind.

From now throughout all lifetimes,
Hold me with your glory.
May I attain unobstructed intelligence
Of great wisdom as it is.

Born in a lotus forest
With the honey of extraordinary qualities of lineage and body,
Praised as a hundred-petaled lotus,
May you care for me always.

May you and your sons
Always hold me so that I may follow you.
With your endless renown and glory,
May you always sustain me.

Excellent display of the melody of supreme youthful rejoicing,
Those who see you, hear you, and chant to you
All see your face.
May you guide us to follow you.

By the virtue of praising you in this way,
The intelligence of all sentient beings is perfected,
Attaining the supreme state of the melodious wisdom goddess.
May I fulfill the wish of complete benefit for all sentient beings.

From the noble lotus pond of pure conduct,
The swan of intelligence calls.
By the white wings of the three practices of the teachings,
May all wise sentient beings be happy.

From the expansive ocean of previous learning,
By the great blessing of the glorious goddess,
May the three realms in which all beings are sustained
Until the end of existence be made completely auspicious.

This praise to the melodious wisdom goddess Saraswati, called The Melody of the Youthful Display of Joy, was written by the Inconceivable Poet Who Has Heard Much,[5] at the Jewel Source of the Mountain of Spontaneity.[6]

Praise to Patrul Rinpoche

JAMYANG KHYENTSE WANGPO

Outwardly, you are the Son of the Victorious Ones,[7]
    Shantideva.
Inwardly, you are the saint, the conqueror Shavaripa.[8]
Secretly, you are the supreme sublime being Dug-ngal
    Rangdröl,[9] actual self-liberator of the suffering of
    beings.
Jigme Chökyi Wangpo,[10] I pray to you.

Praise to Mipham Rinpoche

The supreme knowledge of Manjushri, the Lion of Speech,
    is born in your wisdom mind,
Fully perfecting the aspiration prayers of Kuntuzangpo
And accomplishing the enlightened activities of the
    Victorious Ones with their heirs.
I pray to you, Jampal Gyepe Dorje, Omniscient Mipham
    Rinpoche.

Praise to Dudjom Lingpa

KYABJE DUDJOM RINPOCHE

The sole essence of the undeceiving Triple Gems,
The supreme embodiment of all the oceans of Buddhas of
    the three kayas,
The Dharma king of the three realms, holder of the
    Mahasandhi teachings,
Dudjom Lingpa, the one whose whole mandala is the
    annihilation of demon energy, I pray at your feet.
By the realization and liberation of the equal display of
    samsara and nirvana in Dharmata,
May I attain fully enlightened Buddhahood.

TEACHINGS *and* SADHANAS

1 · The Practice of the View, Meditation, and Action, Called "The Sublime Heart Jewel"

The Speech Virtuous in the Beginning, Middle, and End

PATRUL RINPOCHE

NAMO LOKESHVARAYA!

To hear just one drop of the nectar of your name
Fills my ears with the sound of Dharma for many lives.
Wondrous Triple Gems, renowned for your glory,
May you always bring auspiciousness.

I am like the mango fruit of autumn,
The outside seemingly ripened even though the inside is not.
With phenomena like that, I am a fraudulent image of a
    Dharma practitioner.
My mind and Dharma are not integrated, so I can rarely
    speak about Dharma.

Nevertheless, at your reverent request,
Not refusing your persistence, I will speak honestly.
Without concession to the vulgar beings of the kaliyuga,
I am speaking here, and you must listen.

The supreme god of gods,[11] the great sage Shakyamuni,
    the powerful conqueror,
By the path of honesty attained the state of honesty
And honestly showed to beings the honest noble path.
That's why he became renowned as the greatest sage of all,
    isn't it?

Alas! In this degenerate age, the temperament of beings!
Their noble honesty is diminished by the use of deceit.
Therefore, they have crooked minds and crooked speech.
How can we trust those who lure the minds of others?

Alas! Mind is confused by beholding the beings of this
    degenerate age.
Alas! Who can trust what anyone says?
It's like living in a place of violent rakshas.
Consider that, and please be kind to yourself.

In the past, your own mind took birth in this world—
A solitary wandering consciousness, pushed by karma;
Now again, like a single strand of hair removed from butter,
You'll leave everything and go on alone.

It is indispensable to have good intentions for oneself.
It is indispensable to be honest with one's own mind.
By not accomplishing the essence of Dharma for one's own
    benefit,
Doesn't one destroy one's own opportunities?

The actions and intentions of people in the kaliyuga are so
    base;
No one will be helpful, just cunningly deceitful.
It is also difficult for one to benefit others,
So isn't it better to cut off connections to being busy?

However much superiors are served, they are never satisfied.
However much inferiors are supported, they are never
    content.
Even though we love others, people rarely reciprocate.
You must understand this situation and have a determined
    mind.

Even learning is of no benefit—it only adds to metaphysical
    debate.
Even becoming an accomplished siddha helps nobody—one
    is just heaped with exaggerated criticism.
Even a high position cannot be sustained—it incites revolt.
You must understand this age of degeneration and be tired
    of it all.

Even if an explanation is given, it is misinterpreted and not
    accepted as true.
Even if your intention is beneficial, candid, and from the
    heart, people take it as the reverse.
Behold this age when crooked-minded people call the
    honest ones crooks.
The rope of expectation must be cut, since no one can bring
    about benefit.

The Victorious One said, "All phenomena are like magic."
But what greater magic is there than the present age?
An enticing magician is performing,
So you must fear the magical ways of defilement.

The Victorious One said, "All speech is like an echo."
But now, much more than an echo, it is a re-echo,
Where words and their meanings contradict each other.
You should become more and more weary of the echo of
    these alluring words.

Whoever you see is not human but an imposter.
Whoever speaks is not speaking truth, but just deceptive
    words.
Now there is no longer anyone to trust,
So remain content to be alone.

If bodily action is in accord with Dharma, everyone objects.
If words are spoken honestly, then everyone gets angry.
Even if one is being pure from the heart, it is considered a
    fault.
Now it is time to hide the self-nature.

Hide your body and stay in a solitary place.
Hide your speech and disengage from conversation.
Hide your mind and only watch your own faults.
That is what's called a hidden yogi.

No one can be trusted, so be disgusted.
Nothing has essence, so be sorrowful.

There's no time to accomplish desires, so give up hope.
If you make these three your permanent companions it will
    be beneficial.

Now happiness is exhausted; there's no time to be happy.
Not wanting unhappiness, end it with Dharma practice.
Happiness or unhappiness, whatever occurs, know that it
    comes from the force of karma.
Now have no expectation or doubt about anyone.

With so much hope toward others, a hopeful mouth smiles
    and smiles.
Wanting more and more, we make elaborate arrangements
    to accomplish this,
And make plans to do this and that in the future with hope
    and fear.
Now, no matter what happens, we won't do this at all.

Even if death comes today, don't regret leaving samsaric
    dharmas.
Even if surviving for a hundred years, where's the joy when
    youth is gone?
Now, whether dead or alive, what good comes from this life?
So therefore, just accomplish Dharma for the next life. That
    is all.

O! My sole lord, treasure of compassion,
Root Guru, Lord Chenrezi,
Your Six Syllables of Dharma are the essence of speech.
There is no source of hope other than you.

All learning is left as intellectual understanding, with no
    benefit now.
All that is done is lost in this life, with no benefit now.
All thoughts become delusion, with no benefit now.
It is time to recite the Six-Syllable Mantra, which is truly
    beneficial.

The undeceiving sole source of refuge is the Triple Gems.
The essence of the Triple Gems is Chenrezi.
So, with unchanging, single-pointed faith in Chenrezi,
    the one who knows,
And with confident determination, recite the Six Syllables.

Compassion is the root of the Mahayana path.
Vast compassion is the only path of all the Buddhas.
Compassionate mind is inseparable from the noble path.
From the state of compassion for sentient beings, recite the
    Six Syllables.

From beginningless time until now, we have wandered in
    samsara.
Since whatever was done became negative, wandering in
    existence ensued.
With remorse, confess transgressions with heartfelt
    conviction.
From the state of the four perfect powers,[12] recite the Six
    Syllables.

This attached, grasping mind is the cause of samsara.
Therefore, offer up to sublime beings and give down to
     pitiful beings all accumulations including virtues,
     wealth, and body.
Dedicate samsara and enlightenment to all beings.
From the state of discarding self-cherishing, recite the Six
     Syllables.

The essence of all Buddhas is the Lord Guru,
The protector whose kindness is much greater than that of
     all Buddhas.
The Root Guru and Chenrezi are inseparable.
Have strong, enthusiastic faith and recite the Six Syllables.

Purifying obscurations, meditating on the path, the four
     kayas are realized.
Chenrezi is the holder of the four empowerments.[13]
If your mind is understood to be the Root Guru, the four
     empowerments are complete.
Spontaneously attaining self-empowerment, recite the Six
     Syllables.

Samsara is just self-phenomena, nothing else.
If it is known that all existent phenomena are the deity, this
     benefits others perfectly.
The pure appearances of the four empowerments are given
     to beings instantaneously.
From the state of stirring samsara's depths, recite the Six
     Syllables.

Various systems of visualization cannot all be contained
within the mind;
Meditating on one Buddha is abiding in the unceasing
nature of all Buddhas.
Whatever appears is the enlightened form of Chenrezi, the
Great Compassionate One.
From the unceasing nature of the deity's body of empty
appearance, recite the Six Syllables.

The mantra recitations of reliance, accomplishment, and
activity[14] are only elaborations.
Synthesized as they are, the Six Syllables are the sound of
the Dharma.
All sounds are inseparable from the enlightened speech of
Chenrezi.
By knowing this empty sound as mantra, recite the Six
Syllables.

If conceptions of the two obscurations[15] are purified, then
experience and realization naturally increase.
If self-phenomena are conquered, then enemies and
obstructors are naturally subdued.
Chenrezi is the one who grants common and supreme
attainments in this life.
From the state of the spontaneously present four activities,[16]
recite the Six Syllables.

Dedicate the torma of whatever arises to the guests of
    simultaneous liberation and arising.
Mold the tsa-tsa[17] of empty appearances from the earth of
    whatever phenomena arise.
Offer the nondual prostration to the object of refuge, the
    nature of mind.
From the state of the perfection of all Dharma activities,
    recite the Six Syllables.

Subdue the enemy of hatred with the weapon of love.
Sustain your relatives, the beings of the six realms, with the
    method of compassion.
Sow the crop of experience and realization in the field of
    faith.
From the state of the fulfillment of this life's activities, recite
    the Six Syllables.

Burn this old corpse of attachment in the fire of
    nonattachment.
Guide the seven periods[18] of this present phenomena with
    the essence of Dharma.
Dedicate the accumulated merit of the food for the corpse,
    presented as a smoke offering.
From the state of completing the virtue of the deceased,
    recite the Six Syllables.

Put the son of faith in practice at the door of Dharma.
Be like a reluctant son-in-law with repulsion toward the
    wife's house of this life's phenomena.[19]

Give the daughter of compassion to the bridegroom of the
    three realms.
From the state of the fulfillment of this life's goals, recite the
    Six Syllables.

Limitless phenomena are delusion, never the truth.
Samsara and nirvana are just conceptions, nothing else.
If the arising and liberation of concepts are understood, the
    stages of the path are complete.
By this pith of liberation, recite the Six Syllables.

In the unceasing Dharmakaya nature of the natural mind of
    empty awareness,
If abiding in the uncontrived continuity, self-luminosity
    arises.
Doing nothing, ultimate truth is upheld.
Just leave naked empty awareness fresh, and recite the Six
    Syllables.

While in stillness, cut the movement of thoughts that follow.
From the state of movement, watch the natural face of
    stillness.
There is no difference between stillness and movement, so
    sustain fresh ordinary mind.
With the experience of single-pointed awareness, recite the
    Six Syllables.

By examining relative truth, establish absolute truth.
By establishing absolute truth, watch how relative truth
    appears.

The two truths are indivisible as original awareness, free
    from the intellect.
From the state of the view free from elaboration, recite the
    Six Syllables.

Upon appearances, cut the mind's attachment.
Upon the mind, let the innermost deception of appearances
    collapse.
The inseparability of appearances and mind, completely free
    of duality's trap, is the great pervasiveness.
From the state of the realization of one taste, recite the Six
    Syllables.

The nature of mind is liberated in unending empty
    awareness.
In the self-display of awareness, thought purifies itself.
From the state of sole oneness, mind and awareness are
    inseparable.
Abide in the unceasing nature of Dharmakaya without
    meditation; recite the Six Syllables.

If the appearance of form is recognized as the deity, it is the
    pith of the developing stage.
Attachment to beautiful and ugly appearances liberates
    itself.
Appearances of the mind, free of attachment, are the
    enlightened body of the sublime one, Chenrezi.
From the state of the naturally liberated appearance of
    seeing, recite the Six Syllables.

If the appearance of sound is recognized as mantra, it is the
pith of mantra recitation.
Attachment to pleasing and displeasing appearances
liberates itself.
The wisdom speech of the Six Syllables, free of attachment,
is the self-sound of samsara and enlightenment.
From the state of the naturally liberated appearance of
hearing, recite the Six Syllables.

If the appearance of scent is recognized as unborn, it is the
pith of the completion stage.
Attachment to the appearance of fragrant and foul scents
liberates itself.
All scents, free of attachment, are the morality of the
sublime ones.
From the state of the naturally liberated appearance of scent,
recite the Six Syllables.

If the ganachakra of all tastes is recognized, it is the pith of
offering.
Attachment to what is delicious and distasteful liberates
itself.
Food and drink without attachment are the substances that
please the sublime ones.
From the state of the naturally liberated appearance of taste,
recite the Six Syllables.

If the essence of the equanimity of the appearance of all
feeling is understood, it is the pith of balance.
Appearances of being full, hungry, hot, and cold liberate
themselves.
Outer and inner sensations of feeling, free of attachment, are
the effortless activity of the deity.
From the state of the naturally liberated appearance of
feeling, recite the Six Syllables.

If it is known that all phenomena are empty, this is the pith
of the view.
Concepts of attachment to true and false judgments liberate
themselves.
In the nature of Dharmakaya, all phenomena that exist in
samsara and enlightenment are free of attachment.
From the state of the naturally liberated gathering of
conceptions, recite the Six Syllables.

Do not follow the object of hatred; just watch the grasping
mind of anger.
In the nature of clear emptiness, the self-arisen appearance
of anger liberates itself.
Mirror-like wisdom is not other than clear emptiness.
From the state of naturally liberated hatred, recite the Six
Syllables.

Do not grasp the object of pride; just watch the grasping
mind of pride.
In the nature of primordial emptiness, self-arisen prideful
grasping liberates itself.

The wisdom of equanimity is not other than primordial
    emptiness.
From the state of naturally liberated pride, recite the Six
    Syllables.

Do not pursue the object of desire with attachment; just
    watch the mind of attachment.
In the nature of empty bliss, the self-arisen attachment to
    appearances liberates itself.
Discerning wisdom is not other than empty bliss.
From the state of naturally liberated desire, recite the Six
    Syllables.

Do not follow the object of jealousy; just watch the
    examining mind of jealousy.
In the nature of empty mind, self-arisen examination
    liberates itself.
The wisdom of all-accomplishing activity is not other than
    empty mind.
From the state of naturally liberated jealousy, recite the Six
    Syllables.

Do not elevate the object of ignorance; just watch your own
    nature.
In the nature of empty awareness, self-arisen thought
    liberates itself.
Dharmadhatu wisdom is not other than empty awareness.
From the state of naturally liberated ignorance, recite the Six
    Syllables.

Primordial emptiness-form is unborn like the sky.
Sole empty awareness is Chenrezi.
There is no other Sublime King of the Sky.[20]
Being in the view of emptiness, recite the Six Syllables.

Like a lasso, feeling binds subject and object.
Realizing nondualistic equanimity is Chenrezi.
There is no other Sublime Meaningful Lasso.[21]
While realizing equal taste, recite the Six Syllables.

Perceiving phenomena as real is deluded mind.
Holding all sentient beings with compassion is Chenrezi.
There is no other Sublime One Who Empties Samsara by
    Stirring It from the Depths.[22]
Being in aimless compassion, recite the Six Syllables.

With intention, one wanders in the cycle of the six realms of
    samsara.
Realizing that samsara and enlightenment are the same is
    Chenrezig.
There is no other Great Compassionate One Who Tames
    Beings.[23]
Naturally benefiting others in one taste without
    discrimination, recite the Six Syllables.

If the natural aspect of the eight consciousnesses of ordinary
    mind[24]
Is realized as Dharmakaya sole mind, it is Chenrezi.
There is no other Sublime Ocean of Victorious Ones.[25]
Knowing one's own mind as Buddha, recite the Six Syllables.

To grasp the phenomena of the body as substance is the
    cause of being bound.
To know emptiness-phenomena as deity is Chenrezi.
There is no other Sublime Khasarpani.[26]
In emptiness-phenomena, the form of the deity, recite the
    Six Syllables.

To grasp the phenomena of speech as sound is the cause of
    delusion.
To know emptiness-sound as mantra is Chenrezi.
There is no other Sublime Roar of the Lion.[27]
Recognizing all sounds are mantras, recite the Six Syllables.

To grasp the phenomena of mind as real is the cause of
    delusion.
To remain in the conceptionless nature is Chenrezi.
There is no other Sublime Resting in Sole Mind.[28]
Being in the sole mind of Dharmakaya, recite the Six
    Syllables.

All existing phenomena are primordially pure, the nature of
    Dharmakaya.
Seeing the stainless self-face of Dharmakaya is Chenrezi.
There is no other Sublime Lord of the Universe.[29]
Abiding in all-pervading pure phenomena, recite the Six
    Syllables.

Sole Deity, Chenrezi, is the synthesized essence of all
    Buddhas.

Sole mantra, the Six Syllables, is the synthesized essence of
all mantras.
Sole Dharma, the enlightened mind, is the synthesized
essence of all developing and completion.
From the state of knowing one and liberating all, recite the
Six Syllables.

What is the benefit of having done so much, since whatever
one does causes samsara?
Look at the meaningless nature of whatever we have done.
Now it is better to let go in the state of nothing to do.
Forget all activities; recite the Six Syllables.

Why talk, since all that is said is meaningless?
See how this makes no connection and creates meaningless
distractions.
Now it is better to abide in speechlessness.
Absolutely stop talking; recite the Six Syllables.

Why come and go, since going and staying only cause
fatigue.
With all your wandering, look how you distance yourself
from Dharma,
Now it is better to relax the mind, single-pointedly.
Be at ease; recite the Six Syllables.

What is the benefit of eating? It is only the cause of shit.
Look how much we eat, but still we're never satisfied.

Now it is better to be nourished by the food of samadhi.
Just be done with eating and drinking, and recite the Six
    Syllables.

What is the use of so much thought? It only causes delusion.
Look at your wishful thinking—it never succeeds.
Now it's better to cut short the stream of ideas for this life.
Completely stop thinking; recite the Six Syllables.

What is the use of being rich and attached to wealth?
See how all that's acquired is abandoned at death.
Now it is better to sever attachment to self-fixation.
Quit trying to collect and hoard; recite the Six Syllables.

What is the good of sleeping? It is only a continuation of
    ignorance.
See how life is wasted by just waiting around.
Now it is better to increase diligence from the heart.
Abandon distractions day and night; recite the Six Syllables.

No time, no time to be lax.
If the Lord of Death suddenly arrives, what will you do?
It is better to try to accomplish Holy Dharma right now.
Immediately and with haste, recite the Six Syllables.

Why count the days, months, and years?
Look at changes from moment to moment.
Each of these moments brings us closer to death.
From now, just now, recite the Six Syllables.

Life just goes further and further like the sun to the West.
The Lord of Death comes closer and closer like a shadow.
Now the rest of this life is like the shadow of the setting sun.
There is no more time to remain idle, so recite the Six
     Syllables.

Even though the Dharma of Six Syllables is sublime,
If recited with distracted eyes and mouth, it won't help you.
Attachment to counting mantras is the habit of strong
     grasping at reality.
Single-pointedly look at mind and recite the Six Syllables.

If we examine our own mind again and again,
Whatever we do becomes the pure path.
This alone is the essence of hundreds of precious teachings
All rolled into one; recite the Six Syllables.

At the beginning, this is the speech of sadness at the actions
     of kaliyuga beings.
This speech is advice that I give from myself to myself.
These lamenting words changed my heart deeply.
Thinking you feel the same as I do, I offer them to you.

If your feelings differ from mine and you have the confidence
     of a high point of view and meditation,
Being intelligent with sophisticated worldly traditions and
     Dharma activities,
And relying on plans of big organizations to benefit yourself
     and others—
If this is how you are, then I must apologize to you.

In the middle, to establish the point of view and meditation,
Even though I do not have the experience of realization,
Through the precious lineage of the all-knowing father and
    son,[30]
I expressed what I have understood of their cherished
    enlightened speech.

At the end, this is the speech of renunciation that invokes
    the Dharma.
Although there was no reason to speak these words, they
    happened on their own.
However, it does not contradict the speech of the Buddhas
    and Bodhisattvas.
If you can practice this, that will be very kind.

This speech, virtuous in the beginning, middle, and end,
In the Cave of Accomplishment, White Rock Victorious
    Point,
Was written at the request of an insistent dear friend, unable
    to be patient,
By a ragged man flaming with the five passions.[31]

Although it is uncertain if this is only idle chatter,
The sublime meaning in the unconfused flow of
    accumulated virtue,
For you, for me, and for all sentient beings of the three
    realms,
I dedicate to the cause of fulfilling all aspirations in
    accordance with Dharma.

2 · Mindfulness, the Ocean of Qualities

RIGDZIN JIGME LINGPA

Prostrations to the All-knowing Ones.

The Dzogchen[32] Master Rangjung Dorje,[33] with devotion to the Three Jewels and weariness with samsara, was once staying in the sacred mountain retreat of the glorious Deathless Valley[34] with secret samadhi practitioners who had abandoned the world. Gelong Lama, from the chain of southern peaks in East Bhutan[35] where the rocky slopes of the mountains are covered with forest, respectfully made this request:[36]

"I entered the door of the Holy Dharma at the age of thirteen. In Central and Western Tibet,[37] I studied branches of the arts and sciences and was ordained as a novice and monk. I learned to perform rites from the speech of Vajradhara,[38] the hidden treasures,[39] the eight sections of the mandala,[40] and so on, as well as some others. I also received teachings on the commentaries of the essential tantras. I learned a little about the drawing and measurements of the Do, Gyu,[41] and other mandalas, and many ritual activities.

"Then, renouncing the world and fervently practicing austerities, I meditated in remote mountain retreat for many years. From excessive completion stage meditation that I did not do correctly, the crown center of my head opened and I nearly passed on. Because I kept mindfulness too tightly, obstacles of vital air energy also occurred. In order to develop my practice, I communicated with and sought the advice of many noble Lamas, meditators, and fellow Dharma friends, yet no one except you[42] has shown me the natural understanding of instantaneous mindfulness, which is the essence of meditation.

"Some time ago, while looking through *The Treasure of the Supreme Vehicle*,[43] I had greater devotion than ever before to the Conqueror Longchenpa.[44] I had seen the prediction that an emanation of Vimalamitra would teach the extraordinary view of Dzogpa Chenpo every hundred years, so I had always prayed to hear this. I realized that all my previous hardships were only rigidity. Now that you have introduced the inexpressible, inherently born view to me, is it right just to abide in that natural mind with only mindfulness?"

Gelong,[45] you should know that the root of all Dharma depends on mindfulness. As Lord Nagarjuna[46] said:

> Mindfulness, as it has been realized by sublime beings
>   with wisdom body,
> Is revealed as the only path to Buddhahood.
> Therefore, one should be very careful to focus on and
>   protect mindfulness,
> Because all Dharma will fall if mindfulness fades.

If there is no mindfulness, the activities of hearing, contemplating, and meditating become impossible; even worldly matters cannot be accomplished. By forgetting, even the purpose of all the work of samsaric phenomena named by habit fails. By forgetting, objects are lost. By forgetting, there is delay. At a worldly level, insanity, deluded perception, being haunted by demons, and the inability to retain the meaning of words—all are said to be due to the negative results of faded mindfulness.

If the activity of the path of enlightenment is considered, without first remembering the difficulty of obtaining a precious human body, there cannot be any auspicious, interdependent circumstances in which to meet Dharma. Furthermore, even if one enters the path of Dharma through the force of incidental circumstances, one immediately turns back through lack of mindful awareness of the Buddha's teaching, and also through not remembering from the heart the impermanence of life. When the importance of death is forgotten, everything that is done is lost because it is only for the purposes of this short life. Therefore, because the mind is in an indifferent stupor, the cause and result of the ten nonvirtuous actions that should be abandoned and the ten virtuous actions[47] that should be accepted are forgotten, so the fear of the suffering of samsara and the inspiration of the benefits of liberation are not remembered. The mind is completely distracted by worldly activities and the duties of home. Pride arises from these concerns, and one loses and forgets the meaning of future lives, just like an intoxicated fool.

Regarding this, it is said in *The Sutra of the Ornament of Qualities:*[48]

> For example, there was a man who became drunk and angry. That man could not even find his home or find his way. He was not even aware of his parents, wife, sons, and daughters, and did not remember the Buddha, Dharma,

and Sangha. Because of the intoxicating power of the wine, he was not even afraid to be in a cemetery, thinking, "What is there to fear from so-called gods, nagas, and yakshas?" Likewise, one can be intoxicated by attachment to worldly life and totally deluded by staying at home. Those who are intoxicated by distraction do not search for the Buddha, Dharma, and Sangha, and do not think about being generous, being reborn in the higher realms, or becoming a noble king. By not seeking to be born in the Buddhafields and by wandering in the endless circle of samsara, the sufferings of the hell realm, the animal realm, and the world of the Lord of Death will be experienced.

As this sutra says, when the next life is forgotten, one cannot remember to give alms. Even if one has immeasurable wealth, if one cannot remember to use it for merit, one goes empty-handed when one dies. For example, even at the time of being in the presence of Lord Buddha, who is like precious land,[49] the mother from Lower Waters[50] neglected that opportunity to gain merit through worship. Because of the karma of miserliness, she was reborn as a hungry ghost.

Therefore, when hearing about the qualities of Dharma, from that point on, the mind can be placed in full awareness by giving, great giving, and total giving, so that the power of the mind becomes stronger and stronger until everything has been given. In order to lead others on the path of Dharma, sadness and weariness can be conquered by remembering the meaning of particular Mahayana and Vajrayana vows. Even when seeing and hearing about others who are frightened, one should remember, "I am a Mahayana Buddhist," and then should give them refuge through many skillful means. Or, if one cannot actually do this through one's own power, one can still have compassion and take their immeasurable burden of suffering upon oneself.

When mindfulness has faded, one cannot have either compassion or realization, even though one considers oneself to be a Mahayana Buddhist. Some say they have realization, but their compassion cannot be aroused. Though they may have some understanding of Buddha's teaching, this is a definite sign of not having any realization. As Phadampa[51] said:

> Without compassion, realization cannot be born.
> Fish are in water; they are not on dry land.

It is so true.

Also, morality that has faded comes from not remembering to be ashamed and not having awareness. If one remembers to prevent what should be abandoned of body, speech, and mind, and to collect what should be accepted of the correct, virtuous dharmas by being ashamed of acquiring a bad reputation and of cheating one's teachers, the vows to work for the benefit of sentient beings are not broken.

Through decreasing mindfulness, even someone like Gelong Dri-me Ö[52] was deluded by the potions and powers of a prostitute, so his morality was ruined. After regaining his mindfulness, however, he felt deep regret. Weeping, he related the story to his fellow monks, and they took him to Manjushri to have his sins purified. Manjushri took him to Buddha. Buddha introduced the nature of absolute truth to him, and he realized the truth of the sublime view.

Absolute truth has been explained in many relative teaching sutras and absolute teaching sutras, such as *The Finger Rosary Sutra.*[53] Yet ultimately, if all teachings are completed, then what should be abandoned[54] and its antidote, what should be accepted,[55] are automatically self-purified by wisdom. Then the essential transformation of the Hinayana, Mahayana, and Vajrayana vows can be known.

Thus, the basis of the three vehicles[56] is the vows, and the basis of all vows is the mind. The vows of the three levels of teaching[57] corresponding to the three lineages[58] exist in the mind, ornamented by the different rituals of abandonment and their antidotes. When the three vows[59] are accompanied by extraordinary method and the wisdom of actual liberation, then there is no going, no coming, no remaining, no increasing, and no decreasing whatsoever within the relative appearance of vows, because there are no obstacles to prevent the truth from being seen, and so the essential transformation is accomplished.

It is said in *The Sutra of Completely Clear Intelligence:*[60]

A monk practitioner who has various conceptions about moral discipline, losing moral discipline, and protecting moral discipline will experience the pleasures of the god realms and then wander again in the lower realms of samsara. If someone does not have either the pretension of keeping vows or not keeping vows, there is no conception.

So it is said. This is the pure morality of enlightenment.

Nevertheless, even though vows and moral discipline are spoken of like this, the Great Mendicant from Kashmir considered those who hold the twelve qualities of practice[61] to be living according to the Buddha's teachings from the Tripitaka.

Also, for the important purpose of preventing the misuse of vows, Atisha[62] prohibited the higher secret empowerments for monks because of the circumstances of time and place. Those who practice the siddha activities of secret mantra but only with devotion should also accept this as the absolute teaching.

Those who dispute intellectually, who are eager to insult other doctrines, who are clever only with words, or who refrain from only a single false activity, such as keeping their celibacy mainly out of false pride, are only protecting their vows up to the first layer of foreskin. With their own words and the ego of moral superiority, they have misinterpreted the teachings of the great guides who see the true meaning of the uncontrived essential nature. They change the extraordinary, absolute teaching of the supreme Vajradhara into their own ordinary, relative meaning. These intellectual philosophers cannot understand the essence beyond the limits of their own minds, but all sublime beings who have the qualities of the accomplishments of abandonment and realization,[63] all Buddha activities, siddha actions,[64] and the ability to perform miracles are the same as Buddha. The self-accomplished Vidyadhara Padmasambhava was perceived as the true second Buddha by all those who were honest and wise in the Snow Mountain Ranges. And beyond at the river Ganges, the incomparable great siddha Saraha said:

> Until yesterday,[65] I was not a fully ordained monk.
> From today, I am. The superior monk is a glorious
> Heruka.

If the essential transformation of vows cannot be remembered from these truth-revealing words, and one continues to say that a fully ordained monk, skilled in the Tripitaka, exceeds Vajradhara in the three disciplines,[66] then this would be a new conclusion that has never been uttered before. This would deprecate the supreme, pure-result stage of accomplishment of the unequaled Vajrayana. Furthermore, those who speak in this way break their own vows by distorting whatever behavior they indulge in as well, so refrain from this.

By remembering the inconceivable truth of the absolute nature, it should be understood how to join it with skillful means, because those who have perfectly accomplished siddha actions of Vajrayana practice do not hold the Hinayana point of view.

From the sutras:

> Manjushri, it is like this. For example, when the newborn king of birds, the kalapingka,[67] is in the broken egg, even before coming out of the shell, the kalapingka still naturally sings its beautiful song. Manjushri, likewise, when a Bodhisattva remains in the egg of ignorance, even though he has not conquered the belief in the existence of a self and even though he is not released from the three realms of existence, he still sings the sound of emptiness, the sound of characteristiclessness, the sound of nonwishing, and the sound of not collecting fabrications; and the sound of Buddha Dharma is revealed. Manjushri, it is like this. If the kalapingka goes among peacocks, he will not sing the kalapingka song. Only if he is among kalapingkas will he sing the kalapingka song. Manjushri, in this way,

a Bodhisattva will not teach the inconceivable sounds of Dharma among practitioners of Hinayana and Pratyeka-buddhas, but when he goes among the Bodhisattvas, he will reveal the inconceivable sounds of Buddha Dharma.

Thus it is said that great Bodhisattvas should understand the essence of the vehicle as explained predominantly in the Vinaya according to the six extremes[68] and four methods.[69]

A monk who considers entering the path and takes the three vows should keep each one individually. He should guard the different aspects of each of the vows without mixing them. If he combines the vows, he should bring the lower vow up to the higher vow. If he breaks the vows and needs to correct them, he should do so according to each of the three individual doctrines[70] and instructions. Then he will be able to restore the broken vows. If, however, he does not do this with awareness and mindfulness of the instructions, he will not be able to restore the purity of his vows. For example, from the *Bodhicharyavatara*:[71]

> Those who wish to keep the vows
> Should watch their minds very carefully.
> If the mind is not watched,
> The vows cannot be kept.

It is also said there:

> Those who wish to watch the mind
> Must make every effort
> To guard mindfulness and awareness.
> I join my hands in request that they may all do so.

Also, if mindfulness is impaired, the armor of patience is flawed. Even if one has the ability to endure the harm inflicted by enemies, this armor [of patience] will be broken if there is no mindfulness at the same time that an obstacle is encountered. Before an incident is over and what has happened cannot be changed, it must be instantly remembered, "These harmful beings are controlled by passions. If I did not exist, there would be no cause for them to harm me, because when there is no object to harm, how can there be anyone who harms? The skandhas, elements, and sense gatherings are root circumstances, and the favorable or adverse qualities such as the unmindful behavior of body and speech are contributing circumstances, making me become a target that can be harmed by others. Others are responsible for this and cannot be blamed. I myself took this karmic body, was born in such and such a country, was given this name by parents, and reside in this place. These skandhas come from me and my grasping mind." Remember this and do not reflect on the faults and behaviors of others.

It is said in *The Teachings of Great Compassionate Mind*:[72]

The patience of practicing and the patience of comprehending Dharma are two things to remember.

First:

Even if beings come again and again to a most brave Bodhisattva and insult him, say unpleasant things, use obscene language, or throw rocks and beat him with weapons, the bodhichitta of that perfect Bodhisattva will not be even slightly disturbed, and he will not experience any ill will toward them, wishing to accomplish the transcendent activity of patience. He will have compassion for those sentient beings and say to himself, "Alas, generally these sentient beings are tormented by the karma of their passions. I should not allow any negative conception toward them to arise in my mind. This harmful activity has occurred because I have taken these hostile skandhas." Thus it is said in order to increase compassion for all beings.

So it is said. Second:

If one's own mindfulness has been distracted toward the power of delusion, and if these deluded phenomena mix with the object of perception, then the imagination can create the idea that it is the object that is harmful and increase the power of this association between the object and one's deluded phenomena. As an antidote to this, it is thought, "If these sentient beings do not even exist in absolute truth, then who is there to abuse me, say unpleasant things, use obscene language, or throw rocks and beat me with weapons?" As it says, "I, and all sentient beings, and life, and going, and surviving, and so on, and all compounded phenomena are illusory, empty gatherings and essenceless, like the sky."

Everything should be perceived as having compounded and magical characteristics.

In regard to praise and blame, ignorant beings do not naturally know how to praise others even though they see their positive qualities. They are not sure whether to blame others even when they see their negative qualities. Instead, they are conceited, and the only sound from their mouths is unpleasant blurting. Also, they probably cannot bear to see the wealth and perfect qualities of others, which disturb them. When a Bodhisattva is on the Bodhisattva path, he helps those who wish to be his servants and friends to enter the gate of Dharma, and they learn Mahayana teachings and the profound rituals of Vajrayana from him. However, others who are overpowered by emotions may denigrate the Bodhisattva in many ways. As it is told in the history of Patient Sage,[73] especially our Buddha did not lure anyone for the purpose of gain or attachment, neither tricking others with wealth nor bewitching them with mantras or anything else.

But when the time ripens to subdue beings, the power of wisdom phenomena is victorious. As it is said in *The Great Skillfulness Sutra:*[74]

> When a Bodhisattva practices Bodhisattva activities, he can take young girls into his service in order to completely bring them to liberation. And so it was that having stayed in the home of the Bodhisattva, forty-two thousand girls were brought to the result of enlightenment.

Thus it is also said.

The low-caste girl Noble Body,[75] who expressed desire for Ananda,[76] was ordained as a nun. Disregarding the truth of this, the people from Shravasti[77] created gossip about the two that was never true.

Also, Stainless Renown[78] appeared as an ordinary layperson in order to subdue beings by intelligent skillful means, yet he was inconceivably wise with a history of measureless qualities. Even the two excellent disciples of Buddha could not be compared to him. As with these saints, the Bodhisattva activity of subduing measureless beings cannot be understood by ordinary beings. So therefore, pitiful and unguided sentient beings will have no refuge if Bodhisattvas are not particularly tolerant toward these situations that cause denigration.

Some people think of themselves as great or holy, as described in *The Precious Gathering:*[79]

> A woman from Mon is not seen;
> What is seen is her coral.[80]

Thus, as this example shows, these people try to receive as many teachings as they can without having devotion and reverence. Raising their heads proudly, they conceal the identity of the Lama from whom they received instructions on the positive qualities of abandonment and realization as though he were an outcast. Since this will become a great obstacle to their accomplishment, one should have even more compassion for them and keep a vow of patience toward their ingratitude. Also, the patience of incisive thinking about Dharma comes from remembering the Three Jewels. The patience of enduring hardships develops from remembering the stories of the previous lives of Lord Buddha and the life histories of supreme beings. One must resolve to remember these examples. Likewise, whatever work is done in the Dharma must be joyfully continued with mindfulness or concentration, which is the essence of diligence.

When Buddha was about to pass into parinirvana, he held the hand of Ananda and said:

> Protect the treasure of my precious Dharma with strong aspiration, diligence, and conscientiousness.

As he said, strong aspiration means remembering whatever the aim is again and again; diligence is actually engaging in the aim; and being conscientious is the way that one engages in that aim. This is because all the teachings of the Buddha should be a support to a mind that is completely weary of worldly matters.

As it is advised in *The Sutra of Applying Mindfulness*:[81]

> Monks, meditate in solitary mountain places, caves, cemeteries, and roofless places, seated on a heap of grass. Do not remain in carelessness, so that you have no regret later, at the time of death. This is my advice to all of you.

Thus he revealed his last words.

If there is no mindfulness, there is no support for either diligence or conscientiousness. Even if someone has the armor of diligence like King Ashoka[82] or the three ancestral rulers,[83] whose courage was like a covering of sky over the earth, antidotes must be used to maintain this diligence on the path. Mindfulness is thinking this way persistently without discouragement, conflict, or self-satisfaction, and using these antidotes to laziness.

Without mindfulness, work will take longer or never even be completed because of enemies, demons, thieves, or the changes in life. So therefore, all fading of mindfulness causes a fall into the abyss of laziness. It is especially necessary for the practitioner to keep mindfulness and awareness during all of the four activities[84] of daily life.

Before the Buddha passed into nirvana, his disciples asked him four questions:

> "Lord Buddha, after your parinirvana, who will be our teacher? What will be our doctrine? How will we subdue the six undisciplined monks? And while collecting the teachings, how will we put them together?"
>
> Buddha answered, "After my complete parinirvana, your teacher should be mindfulness and awareness. Your doctrine should be pure moral discipline. You do not have to subdue the six undisciplined monks; they will be liberated by themselves. When you have collected all my teachings, put these words at the beginning as the words of the basic subject: "Once I heard thus." At the end, you should put these words of rejoicing: "The Buddha's speech was greatly praised."

Thus he spoke.

We are able to hear Lord Buddha's unbroken speech in this way, "Once I heard thus," because the disciples of Buddha generally listened by abandoning the three faults of the container,[85] the six stains,[86] and the five faults of not retaining the meaning,[87] and especially by having attained the quality of unforgetting memory.

The essence of unforgetting memory is mindfulness. Arya Manjushri said:

> Perfect memory means unfaded mindfulness, undistracted reflection, unobscured intellect, the manifestation of wisdom, and thorough knowledge of how to distinguish between the different terms of all that can be known.

Thus were his words.

Without mindfulness and awareness, if one goes to beg for alms where dogs bite, then one will burn one's own and others' minds through anger and will do great wrong. It is extensively revealed in many sutras how such habits can be abandoned.

From *The Jewel Clouds:*[88]

> Lineage son, when a Bodhisattva sees beings with few root virtues and great suffering, the Bodhisattva makes a firm resolution to go to beg from them, in order to benefit them. While going to beg in villages, cities, or towns, remain firmly in mindfulness and have refined, composed senses that are not distracted, senses that are not elated, and senses that are calm. Do not look beyond the length of a yoke and always remain mindful of the virtuous dharmas. In that way, go to beg. While going from place to place to receive alms, do not walk directly to a rich householder as great and high as a sal tree, or to a village of a Brahmin family as great and high as a sal tree, or to a village of a royal family as great and high as a sal tree. Instead, beg alms until the purpose is fulfilled. Also, keep the first part of the alms for fellow monks, keep the

second part for suffering beings, keep the third part for sentient beings who have fallen into wrong ways, and eat the fourth part oneself. One should eat moderately, remembering to feed inner organisms. Also, one should not go begging with a mind like a thief or a robber. These were the reasons that the Buddha permitted begging, as he told Kashyapa:[89] "Seek alms for the good of all sentient beings, seek food for those who have no food, and release others from grasping at everything. For these reasons, go begging. You should go to a town to bless it in order to empty it of samsara."

Thus it is said. Remember the purpose of the basic characteristics of this teaching.

Generally, the mind fully controls the actions of both body and speech. The overpowering passions of the mind are like an elephant intoxicated by wine. Without just testing it from time to time, train the mind with mindfulness and awareness as an elephant trainer hits an elephant on the head with an iron hook of awareness and ties it with a good strong rope of mindfulness. Then, one will be able to carry the load of teachings and samaya[90] from the Tripitaka up to the ocean of tantras. Having entered the path without obstacles, one will attain the state of all-knowing liberation. Concerning that, from *The State of Activity*:[91]

> If the elephant of mind is let loose,
> It harms with unbearable torment.
> If, in many ways, the rope of mindfulness
> Ties the elephant of mind,

All fears disappear
And all virtues are attained in hand.

And so it is said.

Especially, the essence of samadhi is not different from mindfulness. In this way, the calm stillness[92] of the Bodhisattva stage of the path of enlightenment is beyond the worldly meditation stages of the four worldly meditations,[93] the four formless equanimities,[94] and cessation,[95] although these are supports that lift one upward on the path. These nine stages are the special source of sublime seeing[96] and the essential antidote to the dullness of neutralized extremes, so therefore, they are named meditation. So it is said.

From *The Jewel Clouds:*

> The essence of samadhi itself is the mind abiding one-pointedly.

This characteristic is like a grand archer testing a bow, or like tuning the peg of a lute so the tension of the string remains evenly balanced. Likewise, if one constantly guards mindfulness while meditating on bodhichitta and the visualizations of the developing stage, or while contemplating the essence of the pure nature of appearance in the completion stage, then one will have the sense of what is called samadhi by keeping mindfulness balanced at all times without intervals. Obstacles can be purified to keep this balance, and the antidotes, acceptance and rejection, can be applied. The four antidotes to laziness are faith, aspiration, effort, and refining one's experience; the antidote to forgetfulness is mindfulness;

the antidote to elation and fogginess is awareness; the antidote to excessive effort is relaxation; and the antidote to non-effort is watchfulness.

Though there are six categories of obstacles to this balance, the worst one is the dispersion of forgetting the true nature, which is the essence of simultaneously born ignorance. But if there is mindfulness, the other five categories do not have so much power to hold each of their own characteristics.

All virtues and all actions ultimately fail when mindfulness and awareness have faded through holding on to ignorant mind, as this story illustrates. Once a very strong giant and a gymnast were wrestling. The giant took the gymnast by the neck and threw him on the ground with all his might. The gymnast struggled with the giant by trying various movements of the fourth, third, second, and first techniques. Even though the giant's strength decreased, the gymnast still could not hurt him. Finally, very upset, the gymnast ran home and wept. His wife asked him what was wrong, and he said, "Today I fought with a giant and I was humiliated. If I fight tomorrow, there will be no other choice for me but to die."

Then she answered, "Do not cry; I have a scheme." The next day she followed behind him. While the two men were fighting, she sang, "Giant, though your strength is great, the jewel on your forehead is nearly falling." As she sang this song, three different thoughts occurred to the giant, and so he became distracted. The gymnast grabbed the giant's testicles to overcome him and started to kill him.

Then the giant said, "The giant whose mindfulness and awareness has faded was killed by a weak but careful person. I see no greater enemy or more clever deceiver than distraction of the mind." (Thinking about the jewel is desire; paranoia about losing is anger; not seeing the self-jewel and being desperate is ignorance.) It is told that after saying this, the giant died.

In that way, when the senses are distracted toward objects while meditating with concentration, the rope of mindfulness is broken. Even though a meditator may be knowledgeable about the five sciences,[97] inner awareness can be stolen by the thieves of the undercurrents of conception without being noticed, which may lead one to the city of delusion.

Before Ngog-lo Chenpo[98] passed away in front of Mount Hepori,[99] he said:

> These skandhas, profusely piled one upon the other,
>   are like a mass of foam,
> Deceiving by appearing to be like Mount Meru.

Thus he showed that one cannot progress on the path by only hearing and contemplating without being restored by the wisdom of meditation. The emanation of this great sublime being was predicted in the root tantra of Manjushri, the *Mulamanju Tantra*.[100] He had no ordinary conceptions, but through his extraordinary compassion he spoke in this way for the benefit of other beings.

By the complete gathering of mindfulness, the passions can be overcome and the obviously positive qualities of joy and happiness can develop. From the beginning, the path of accumulation depends on mindfulness. There is also said to be mindfulness on the path of union with the power of mindfulness, on the path of seeing in the first of the seven branches of enlightenment, and on the path of meditation in the seventh of the Noble Eightfold Path. With the development of mindfulness, all the qualities of the five paths manifest. Particularly, the essence of mindfulness is to abide naturally in the wisdom of abiding in nonduality[101] and not to be under the power of elation and dullness. It is named the unity of the samadhi of calm stillness and sublime seeing. This must be done carefully. The mind will become totally distracted if it is practiced with too much effort, and without the antidotes of willingness and mindfulness, sublime seeing will fade. In brief, all virtues in the path of accumulation and the path of union with the mindfulness of effort are gathered from this, so it is called the mindfulness of perception and belongs to the ordinary path. Then, other paths gradually open.

From *The Treasure of the Precious Jewel:*[102]

> Those who are beginning practitioners, do not forget
>   concentration with the mindfulness of perception.
> Those who practice the wisdom of abiding in
>   nonduality and the wisdom after attainment, do
>   not forget the pure nature of appearance.
> Those with refined experience, do not forget the
>   wisdom of the appearance of mindfulness.
> When profound confidence occurs, there is no one who
>   forgets and nothing to forget.
> Completing changelessness, the object of distraction is
>   the pure nature of appearance.
> When phenomena are exhausted, it is beyond
>   indication and speech.
> Until that time, I request that thorough effort be made
>   like this.

So it is said. For that reason, if ascetic meditators establish all the great Dharma sounds of the path into the characteristics of mindfulness, those meditators with keen instantaneous faculties perfect the special, supreme Dharma method of Dzogpa Chenpo without trying to put mindfulness in the state of abiding in nonduality. Mindfulness itself becomes the essence of completely abiding in nonduality, and is the best way to pass through all stages.

Nonetheless, for most people it is difficult to have the right view because they cannot assimilate it due to their karma and merit. Whoever cannot understand the right view and is not taught to sustain mindfulness during meditation becomes scattered and cannot focus the mind in the passage of concentration.

If the first of the two ways of keeping mindfulness[103] is mastered, then mindfulness perfects itself as the essence of abiding in nonduality. So, the object to look at and the one who looks are not different. Even when distracted, the conception itself that distracts is mindfulness, like the inseparability of fire and heat. When conception and mindfulness become one taste in the instantaneous experience of a practitioner with a keen faculty, a definite stage cannot be made.

According to the second way,[104] mindfulness should be tightened during meditation, but when mindfulness goes after a thought while being distracted, it is overpowered by delusion. When mindfulness returns again, one enters the state of abiding in nonduality.

In this way, if the effort is diligently made to bring these states of mindfulness together, then conceptions are just temporary stains, so they are unable to bear the face of mindfulness as mindfulness becomes stronger. It is like fire meeting what is to be burned, or a lamp being raised in a dark hole. Even many arising conceptions cannot affect the state of abiding in nonduality. The essence of the conception itself becomes mindfulness. It is said that rejection is transformed into the antidote itself, and is the power of the mindfulness of perception.

If mindfulness with effort cannot be controlled with diligence, ignorance and the gathering of thoughts increase as much as the power of mindfulness decreases, until ultimately meditation is frustrated. This is illustrated in the example of a greedy herdsman.

Once a very greedy herdsman found a big piece of gold in a deserted place. He was so happy that he even neglected to look after the cattle. Not even remembering to eat, he only held the piece of gold, shifting it from his right hand to his left hand. When he saw some marmots and mice, afraid that they would steal his piece of gold, he sang:

A poor man has no food in his hands.
He who mistakes white rock for butter
Will have tooth trouble.

Thus he sang.

After a few days, some of his cattle tumbled down the mountain and some were taken by wild animals, so most of the herd was lost. The owner of the cattle quarreled with the herdsman. Because of his extreme greed, the herdsman did not even mention what had happened. He pretended to be sick and went to sleep in the surrounding thickets. That night, when cats came to hunt for mice, he thought they were someone who had come to rob him of his piece of gold, so he pondered over a method for using the gold. "If I give this piece of gold to the king of the country, I will become a great householder. Then my wife will give birth to a son who, if he becomes skillful in science and art, will undoubtedly become the king's minister. When this happens, there is no doubt that the piece of gold will come into my hands again." He felt so happy about this that he danced and stomped about. His mind became distracted and the piece of gold fell out of his hands and was lost in the wild thicket. Then he said:

> It is better to have mindfulness than a piece of gold.
> Having lost the wish-fulfilling gem of mindfulness,
> The piece of gold was lost to the hands of the enemy.
> This consciousness without mindfulness
> Ruins everything in this world.

So it was told. This example shows the outer and inner characteristic faults[105] of neglecting one's meditation and being callous through the lack of mindfulness.

Nevertheless, by increasing the positive qualities of mindfulness more and more, the self-exhausting basis of mind is finally reached in the great stage beyond the phenomena of mind. For example, in sculpture, if the clay is not moist at the beginning, no work can be done. But if the moisture does not dry at the end, the purpose of the work cannot be completed.

From *The Pinnacle of the Vajra Point Tantra:*[106]

The moving horse of the mind is bridled with
   mindfulness.
As an elephant is turned by an iron hook,
As a wild horse is subdued by a bridle,
The movement of thoughts is subdued by mindfulness.
When mindfulness becomes completely unobscured, it
   is wisdom.

So it is said.

The supremely realized yogi Phadampa was asked, "When
Buddhahood is attained, then how will this awareness
become?" He replied, "It is wisdom purified of the mind's
conceptions." Then he was asked, "Does wisdom have mindfulness or not?" He answered, "What are you saying? Mindfulness is the intellect of sentient beings. Wisdom is free from
intellect."

For that reason, one must fully conquer the twenty wrong
views by the inconceivable wisdom point of view of the prajnaparamita,[107] which is free of all activity. These wrong views
are viewing form as self, viewing self-form as extraordinary
self-essence, viewing form as having self-essence, and viewing self as having a true essence of form; and in the same
way, [each of the other four skandhas of] feeling, perception,
intention, and consciousness are viewed according to these
four categories.

These twenty wrong views are annihilated by the view of
wisdom, which is free from any extreme. It is through this
wisdom that one then sees all dharmas as being like the sky
and sees beyond the mental activity of claiming their essence

to be empty. This viewing is the meditation of abiding in nonduality beyond worldliness because it is free from the five skandhas. It must be learned how that experience, which is the wisdom of discernment, should permeate all the after-attainment of abiding in nonduality. This is called the uncontrived essential nature of mindfulness. It is the antidote that removes the root of the passions and their residue.

And furthermore, in developing this experience, do not even try to remember or think about wanting to experience subtle discernment, the eight consciousnesses, or the gross stains of conception. Thinking that one is not even supposed to think too much and then thinking excessively, as well as any other obscurations, will be abandoned through the supreme wisdom of conceptionless sublime seeing, which is freedom from the ultimate subtle obscurations and from all points of view.

The *Prajnaparamita* says:

> Whatever is beyond remembering or is inconceivable to the mind is the prajnaparamita.

So it is said. The mindfulness of having attained the actual revelation of this meaning is named the branch of enlightenment of the path itself. It is categorized as the wisdom appearance of mindfulness. If expressed from the precious teachings of the self-essence of Dzogpa Chenpo, since both what should be abandoned and its antidote never exist, there is no mindfulness with conception involved. When self-nature is recognized, there is no need for mindfulness. It is self-liberated, so it cannot be bound again by mindfulness. There is neither basis nor root, so it does not depend on the antidote of

mindfulness. The essence cannot be examined, so the puri-
fier of mindfulness itself is self-purity. Since the power of the
uncontrived essential nature[108] has prevailed, mindfulness is
self-free. Since wisdom is undeluded, there is no focusing on
mindfulness.

Here, from *The Meditation Stage:*[109]

> Even if there is no mindfulness and mental activity, if there
> is no discernment, then how can one enter the stainless
> essence of the appearance of all phenomena? Even though
> all phenomena abide in self-emptiness, emptiness will still
> not be realized without discernment.

So it is said.

Through very different interpretations, some try to establish mindfulness itself as a substantialization of the wisdom
of discernment. By taking that position, many say that those
sublime, indisputably renowned ones in the Snow Mountain
Ranges,[110] who revealed the path and attained the accomplishments of this path through the pure point of view, are not
right. Actually, the pith of the exact center is known only by
the Omniscient Subduer, Buddha. That ultimate state is also
Dharmakaya, whose characteristic is beyond the knowledge
of conceptualization and examination. So, therefore, there is
no intention here to claim that one's point of view is superior,
nor is there enjoyment in denigrating the point of view of
others. But ignorant beings and those who have attachment
to one-sidedness will not have doubt if this is explained a little
with incisiveness.

Whatever the actual, uncontrived state of the self-essence

of the path is, it is seen from the pure wisdom of meditation, as was just sufficiently covered and as will be explained again. In particular, the theories of the Uma Rang-gyupa[111] were erased[112] by the Uma Thalgyurpa.[113] In the text by Atisha called *The Simultaneous Entrance*,[114] it says:

> All tangible form is a gathering of subtle substance. When each aspect of that subtle substance is investigated and analyzed, not even the subtlest substance remains. Furthermore, there is not even the subtlest form or the slightest perception. That which has no form is mind. Even regarding that mind, the past mind has ceased, the future mind has not yet occurred, and the present mind is very difficult to examine. If mind is examined with the weapon of awareness, it is realized that it has no color and is free from form, or that, like space, it does not exist, or that it is free from being one and many, or that it is unborn, or that it is naturally pure light, and so on. It is then realized that mind does not exist. Since in essence both tangible and intangible do not exist, discerning wisdom itself also does not exist. For example, after two pieces of wood rubbed together to cause fire have both been burned, the fire that burned them also ceases. In the same way, since individual or general characteristics do not exist, wisdom is not perceptible and there is only clear light without the condition of the existence of any substantial essence. In this way, all faults of elation and dullness are dispelled. At that time, mind should not think anything or grasp anywhere. Abandoning all mindfulness and mental activity,

one should leave this as it is until signs of the enemy no longer arise as thieving thoughts.

So it is said.

Some doctrines say that since there is mindfulness, there is discernment, and that since there is discernment, there is a subtle holding of a point of view. Theorizing that this is not contradictory to the ultimate state is a great carnivorous demon that will be exorcised by the profound words of the *Prajnaparamita*.

If it is said that there is not even a subtle holding of a point of view in the ultimate state of wisdom, the misinterpretation could be made that the phenomena of mindfulness totally fade like the five mindless states[115] of deep sleep, fainting, and so on, which are mentioned in *The Discernment of Center and Edge*.[116] If it is then asked what the difference is between freedom from mind and these mindless states, it can be answered that the five mindless states are not even generally similar to the essential nature. If the five mindless states are captured by skillful means, then how can they be indifferent stupor? They are not indifferent stupor. Mindfulness and mental activity are categories of what is to be abandoned and its antidotes, which arise in this case from analyzing and examining wisdom, which is the cause of intellect, words, suppositions, contrived examination, all that arises, all characteristics whatsoever, and so on.

Here, by wisdom free from thoughts, Dharmata without mindfulness is seen. By wisdom free from words, the meaning of the sutras is known. By wisdom free from supposition, the state of the essence of abiding is unobscured. By wisdom beyond contrived mind, the basis of mindfulness is exhausted and the wisdom of sublime seeing manifests. By the essence of the wisdom of cutting through that which arises, there is complete freedom from the passions. By the wisdom free of characteristics, conceptionlessness is understood. By opening the door of completely pure, natural, luminous awareness,[117] the basis of all qualities is never obstructed. From that basis come the attainments of wisdom eyes, all-clear knowing, spiritual unforgetfulness, miraculous senses, inexhaustible wish-fulfilling knowledge, and the ten powers.[118]

On the self-path of prajnaparamita, the difference between the Buddha and the Bodhisattvas can be understood from the text named *One Hundred Thousand*:[119]

Rabjor,[120] it is like this. Those who enter the path are different from those who complete the result of the path, but it cannot be said that both are not sublime beings. Rabjor, in this way, brave, great Bodhisattvas have entered the uninterrupted path. Fully enlightened Buddhas[121] have obtained the unobscured wisdom of all dharmas. Rabjor, this is the difference between a brave, great Bodhisattva and a fully enlightened Buddha.

So it is said. And also:

If a Bodhisattva practices the six paramitas and the sixteen kinds of emptiness, and meditates, only then will he attain Buddhahood in the future. A Buddha knows all dharmas with instantaneous wisdom mind, so therefore he is called a fully enlightened Buddha.

For that reason,[122] there is the system of stages of the path and how to attain liberation; of the attainment of bhumis and qualities in the four stages of the path of learning[123] and the fifth stage of no more learning; [124] and of the attainment of the samadhi of the most courageous ones, and so on, by tenth-stage[125] Bodhisattvas who in their after-attainment receive the great light empowerment[126] from Buddha. All of these are true according to the path of whichever yana one is following, so it is better not to hold only one doctrine as true.

Here, all those systems are categorized as actual relative truth from the point of view of the great secret path of the vajra essence. As it is said:

> There is no question that Buddha is mind;
> Even all sentient beings are one's mind.
> The Buddha's teaching is also one's mind
> And therefore they are equal in essence.
> There is no sublime path of absolute truth other than
>   this.

Thus, view and meditation vanish when abiding in the great nature becomes the profound expanse. The doctrine of stages falls away, leaping to the great, spontaneously accomplished wisdom.

In general, according to Dzogpa Chenpo, in the texts that were translated from the Sanskrit there are many instructions on the tantras of the Mind Section[127] (the lineage of the Mind Section is predominantly about the profound expanse), the Expanse Section[128] (the lineage of the Expanse Section is predominantly about the equanimity of space and clarity), and the Precious Teachings Section[129] (the lineage of the Precious Teachings Section is predominantly about clear light). These traditions descended from Vairochana[130] and Nyag[131] (the followers of the lineage of Vimalamitra), and so on.

In early Tibet,[132] the tradition of meditation descending from Nyang Sherab Jungne[133] especially flourished, and there were practitioners renowned for attaining supreme siddhi.[134] (Relying on the secret profound wisdom lineage of the precious, indestructible, continuous bridge, Vairochana taught Mipham Gönpo.[135] From this lineage, many attained rainbow body. Mipham Gönpo taught Nganlam Jangchub Gyaltsan,[136] who taught Zadam Rinchen Yig,[137] who taught Khumgyur Sal,[138] who taught Nyang Jangchub Drag,[139] who taught Nyang Sherab Jungne from Uru Sha,[140] a monk who put his robes and rosary on the branch of a juniper tree from the mountain of deities near the Great Cave and vanished in a wisdom rainbow body.) The tradition of nonmeditation descended from Kor Yeshe Lama.[141] Both of these systems flourished among the disciples of Zurchung Sherab Dragpa.[142]

There was also the tradition from Kham.[143] (The miraculous emanation of the sublime being named Aro Yeshe Jungne[144] appeared in Longthang Dronma.[145] He wrote the text called *Practice of Mahayana*.[146] Atisha was very pleased by this. Then, the fifth lineage holder was Kharag Gomchung.[147] Aro's lineage from India and China was taught up to Chogro[148] and Yazi,[149] both of them seventh lineage holders, who taught the Greatest Scholar, Rongzom Mahapandita.[150]) [The tradition from Kham] descended from Aro Yeshe Jungne or Lama Zur Gongpa Sel[151] (Vairochana, for the first time at Gyalrong Dragla,[152] the holy place of the protectors, taught Yudra Nyingpo,[153] who was the actual lineage holder) and is the tradition of meditation, nonmeditation, and both together. These three lineages were renowned in Tibet.

However, the Conqueror, Omniscient Longchen Rabjam[154]—who is truly worthy to be glorified by the names Enlightened Victor, Great Profound Expanse, and Samantabhadra, and who actually came to the Snow Mountain Ranges and turned the wheel of Dharma—established into one essence all the precious teachings of the three sections[155] on the nature of Dzogpa Chenpo, without regard for outer philosophical conclusions.

Of the methods with meditation, the natural revelation of passing simultaneously to the direct clear light manifestations of Buddhas[156] is said to be superior, and of the ways without meditation, the stainless nature[157] is said to be superior. Those who know the nature of the essence of the different doctrines with characteristics are very rare. Most people basically consider passing simultaneously to be superior and only praise that way.

In general, if the stainless nature is not established, one cannot pass to enlightenment only through the doctrine of spontaneity.[158] It is like farming without land and hoping for a harvest. Why is this? It is because the essential nature of mind, which is abiding in Dharmakaya, has to be established by the natural revelation of cutting through all substantial and insubstantial phenomena[159] without error or delusion. In that state, if one obtains confidence in the three experiences of abiding, stability, and liberation, and then enters into the doctrine of spontaneity, the three inherent kayas self-appear in pure awareness. One does not need to wait for the

Sambhogakaya and its purelands to manifest in the future since they are established as the present phenomena of the path. Therefore, the gross elements are exhausted and transformed into a body of light. But ignorant people do not know the meaning of abiding in natural mind. Also, they do not understand the essential meaning of the energy of awareness mind, which is self-vanishing through practice by giving up all this life's activity in passing simultaneously. Instead, just as long as they survive, they guess with diligence, hope with great longing to see visions even though these are only temporary, and expect to attain rainbow body without any basis of reason whatsoever. Nowadays in this Snow Mountain Range, there are many of these people outrageously in pursuit like this. It is much more effective to make diligent effort on the path based on one's own persistence.

In the doctrine of determination,[160] the basis of the nature of mind does not abide in samsara and nirvana, in existence and nonexistence, or in eternalism and nihilism. It is not activated by any root or contributing circumstances, so therefore it self-manifests as the three doors of liberation.[161] There is no distraction and no one who is distracted.

Regarding this, to define the three correct self-liberations, liberation from the beginning does not rely on any view, activity, meditation, or result of the lower yanas, such as wishing that someday there will be liberation. Self-liberation is not the same as the potential Buddha nature of sentient beings that is covered by sudden stains and by not understanding the Lama's teaching, and is mixed with passions so that delusion cannot be transformed into the pure nature. Here, there is no attachment even to the edges of any of these views.

The essence of liberation is the attainment of the nature of mind itself, which from the beginning has never wandered in samsara and is liberated in profound great space, like a garuda spreading its wings inside the egg. When it has perfected the three skills of the body, the eggshell falls on the ground at the same time as the garuda soars into the sky. Other birds are not capable of flying immediately; only garudas can do this. As with this example, no other way except Dzogpa Chenpo has this quality of giving no regard to the signs of accomplishment of stages and paths.

In *The Great Display*,[162] it says:

> There is no duality of sentient beings and Buddhas,
> So how can the path alter this?

So it was said.

This is the special secret of Dzogpa Chenpo, and it is difficult to fit it into an intellectual mind. It is difficult even for people who consider themselves practitioners of the path of Dzogpa Chenpo to realize it. That is because they say that the meanings of *The Essence of Buddha*,[163] *The Decoration of Magnificent Ornaments*,[164] the *Parinirvana Sutra*,[165] and so on, which are the final Wheel of Dharma, and the meaning of *Sambhuti*,[166] *Hevajra*,[167] *Domjung*,[168] *Shadgyu Dorje Threngwa*,[169] and so on, which are tantric teachings, are in fact identical in true point of view with the *Lankavatara Sutra*.[170] But these people could not discern between Buddha nature with temporary stains that exists in the minds of all sentient beings and what is shown as the stainless wisdom essence that is to be realized.

Some claim to follow our doctrines concerning our view but reject the proper way of connecting the view with Buddha's Dharma of speech and with logic. They continually rely on foolish meditation due to ignorance about the doctrine of the Conqueror, Longchenpa.

Here, when becoming one with space in the right way, the object of distraction is the pure nature. In this case, regarding the essential nature of awareness and the essential nature of phenomena, the first one is emphasized.

Not abiding in delusion, the object of distraction is the pure nature.[171]

Not abiding in limited, nihilist views, the object of distraction is the pure nature.

Not abiding in either having or not having, the object of distraction is the pure nature.

Not abiding in one or many, the object of distraction is the pure nature.

Exhausting the basis of relying on doctrines, the object of distraction is the pure nature.

Purifying the partiality of view and meditation, the object of distraction is the pure nature.

Free from any basis of delusion, the object of distraction is the pure nature.

In great, unending, pure awareness, the object of distraction is the pure nature.

Purifying supposition, the object of distraction is the pure nature.

With no basis of distraction, the object of distraction is the pure nature.

Expansive like the sky, the object of distraction is the pure
nature.
There is no night and there is no day; the object of
distraction is the pure nature.
Meditation and nonmeditation are purified; the object of
distraction is the pure nature.
There is no existence of self-characterized knowledge; the
object of distraction is the pure nature.

Thus, the exhaustion of the wisdom of the pure nature is
beyond description.
So, as there was nothing enlightened, there is no hope for
Buddhahood.
There was nothing that wandered in samsara, so therefore
the idea of sentient beings is abandoned.
By viewing, only one side is seen, so therefore, view and
meditation are just extra activity.
If one comprehends through supposition and contrivance,
there is no progress on the path of spiritual levels.
There is no progress by realization, because awareness mind
is attained as it primordially is.
The result is perfectly complete within the basis, so there are
no faults and there are no positive qualities.
Cause and result, whether high or low, are equal, so happiness
and suffering are exhausted in the pure nature.
There is no duality arising or ceasing, so therefore, there is
only one vast, stainless sphere.

Thus spoken to Gelong Monpa,[172] Latod Choje,[173] Dharmakirti,[174] Padro Kundrol,[175] Khampa Gelong,[176] and so on,

all the disciples who reached the path[177] rejoiced and greatly praised the teachings of the Great Perfection. As of now, advice on mindfulness, the ocean of qualities, is completed.

SWASTI. This speech on mindfulness and awareness is the root of all Dharmas and was given by the All-Knowing Jigme Lingpa, who was a Master of mindfulness. It was printed for the purpose of restoring the mindfulness of the totally deluded and distracted Ling-se Gönwang.[178] By the merit of this, may all mindless sentient beings reach the ultimate state of the continuous river of nondistracted, all-pervading mindful awareness and uncover the pure nature of the wisdom of mindfulness in primordial space where all phenomena are exhausted, the originally pure basis of mindfulness.

3 · The Lion's Roar

Cutting Through the Errors and Deviations of the
One Free from Activity, Meditating on the Heart Essence

RIGDZIN JIGME LINGPA

From the beginning meditationless, unchanging,
    uncontrived,
Undistracted, unholding, having the essence of awareness,
Free from the perception of letting go and retaining because
    of grasping mind,
Prostrations to the Great Perfection by self-sustaining,
    unending natural continuity.
The quintessence of the Great Perfection, the tantric section
    of clear light,[179]
The lotus heart essence that is the red nectar of the wisdom
    dakini's heart,
The meaning that is beyond all the nine yanas,
Is only transmitted by the power of the wisdom mind
    lineage and cannot be put into words.
Nevertheless, for the benefit of practitioners who are settled
    in one-pointed concentration
In the supreme, essential meaning
Without the divisions of rigidity, compulsions, or
    examination,
This is revealed from the treasury of vast, profound mind.

Well, then, here, from the fortunate connections made by the pure prayers of previous lifetimes, one meets a holy Lama who has perfect characteristics and the lineage of realized meaning. If one prays to him with the certainty and trust of belief with strong, one-pointed faith and intention, the realization of the Lama is transmitted to the disciple through the contributing circumstance of devotion. The natural freedom from elaboration of the Great Perfection, which is the way of abiding that cannot be explained through words or examples, is unobstructed and measureless, and does not fall in any direction. This present natural mind that cuts through all phenomena, without shedding like fur or changing color, completely becomes meditation, and by this, the attachment to meditation itself is purified. When one is released from the ties of view and meditation, the insight of confidence is born from within and the knower dissolves into objectlessness. So, there is no benefit from noble conceptions, no harm from ignoble conceptions, and one is not fooled[180] by indifferent stupor. The union of the vast expanse and awareness becomes immense and all-pervasive, the qualities of the path become clearly apparent, and not even the names of deviations, errors, and strayings exist.

Even though this is so and this Dharma is the supreme king of vehicles, there are many variations of superior, lower, or intermediate faculties, and it is very difficult to gather only those with keen faculties. Therefore, the subduer[181] and the subdued[182] misinterpret each other, so even if one meditates, errors arise and it is very difficult to develop qualities. According to the capacity of those who learn gradually, there are three stages in meditation: understanding, experience, and realization. (If it pertains to the general yanas, in the path of accumulation, there is understanding; in the path of union, there is experience; and in the path of sublime seeing, there is realization. That is what many previous sublime beings have said, and it is very true.)

Nowadays, many practitioners grasp at understanding as the pith of meditation and are lost in an imitation of meditation. The way this happens is that when there is the experience of emptiness and clarity without thought, in that relaxed and comfortable state of abiding in nonduality,[183] the experience of bliss predominates. Also, self-righteousness arises: "This is my meditation. Nobody knows better than this. I have such realization." At this time, if one is not guided by a perfect Lama then, as said in the Great Perfection teachings, "Understanding is like a patch that will soon fall off." So it is said.

When good and bad circumstances are met, many practitioners will separate from their practice like water from milk. Even though it is a little easy for some practitioners to carry bad circumstances into practice, it is very difficult to carry good circumstances into practice. Even those who think they have obtained the highest realization are only trying to obtain splendid circumstances in this present life. Everywhere, there are those who are attached to distraction, the demon of the son of the gods,[184] which is the mind that wanders because of not having realization of the essence of the self-liberation of the six sense gatherings. These days, many do not see this as a fault, but rather as a wondrous sign of accomplishment. So therefore, even here, this speaker becomes a white crow.[185]

But meditators who really practice Dharma from the heart, without being satisfied with a dull view of meditation with characteristics, should do four periods of meditation, practice predominantly Guru Yoga with skillfulness, and after taking the four empowerments unite with the mind of the Lama and relax in open awareness. Until the essence of that experience has vanished into aimlessness and sourcelessness, one needs to put a bone in the heart.[186]

Likewise, in experience, there is the experience of great emptiness when calm stillness is predominant, and there is the experience of clear light when sublime seeing is predominant, and so on. To synthesize, even if there are some who understand the faults of the movement of mind, whose discerning awareness wisdom radiates, and who understand how to carry both stillness and movement into meditation, they can still have a tight grasping at the self in the essence of the one who understands. Getting lost in the characteristics of examination, analysis, and so on, is an extremely hidden, serious cognitive obscuration.

So therefore, without hastily giving the name of Dharmakaya to conceptions, there is only unfailing present natural mind, which is unbroken edgelessness. Just carry this freely and transparently onto the path, without depending on the antidote of the meditator and without being bound by attachment to a view. Instead of this, if someone is still lost in examining the understanding of abiding in nonduality and after attaining nonduality,[187] then there is a narrow path on the edge of a precipice of deviations, errors, and ways of straying. If these are not recognized, what is correct and incorrect cannot be distinguished, so these hidden faults are exposed here.

Great emptiness means empty from the beginning, which is egoless and free from the four extremes[188] or the eight extremes of elaborations.[189] Awareness mind is this knowing of nowness.[190] Just recognize this freeness beyond intellectual mind. Not understanding this, if nothingness is considered to be emptiness after examination by the intellect through negating and affirming what is and is not, as in the lower vehicles, or, if one affirms only the clear light emptiness of samadhi and experiences a view of seeing all phenomena as magic-like by purifying everything into emptiness through the mantra SO BHA WA, as in the lower tantras, then this is an error.

Also, calm stillness is the self-pacification of subtle and gross thoughts. The pure nature of mind is free from waves of the ordinary mind of movement. It is the pristine, natural, self-aware, self-clear state of sustaining. Not understanding this, if one thinks of this as remaining in an unconscious, insensate state, this is an error.

Sublime seeing is just this self-radiance of nongrasping clear awareness that recognizes the self-face of both stillness and movement. Not understanding this, there is an error of mistaking it to be the intellect that analyzes and examines stillness and movement.

Even though there are various categorizations of the states of "abiding in nonduality" and "after attaining nonduality," in the Great Perfection's own terms, naturally sustaining the essence of whatever arises recognized by mindfulness is abiding in nonduality. Then, knowing this, sustaining the aspect of the movement of mind such as various manifestations, transformations, and so on, with alertness is the state called "after attaining nonduality." Not understanding this, if one considers remaining one-pointedly in the emptiness of staring to be abiding in nonduality, and arising from that state, if one imposes an imitation of emptiness as an illusion and calls it "after attaining nonduality," this is an error.

Nondistraction means not being lost in subtle undercurrents of delusion or indifferent stupor; it is immaculate, unending mindfulness. Not understanding this, if one is fearful and cautious about being distracted and is bound by a repressed, constricted mind, this is an error.

Natural, ordinary mind means this present mind unstained by either faults or good qualities. This self-nature is sustained by the continuity of awareness. Not understanding this, if one grasps at the substantiality of the rigid concepts of worldly, ordinary mind, this is an error.

To be meditationless means to enter profound, unconditioned natural space, detached from meditating and non-meditating, without any contrivance or aim, stabilizing the expansive fortress of mindfulness. Not understanding this, if one remains in ordinary, careless neutrality, or is lost in meaningless indifference, this is an error.

To sustain whatever arises means to directly watch whatever thoughts arise, without rejecting, without examining, and without following, but releasing them into the self-awareness of the one to whom they arise, transparently sustaining both stillness and movement. Not understanding this, just following after and analyzing whatever conceptions arise is an error.

As for the three deviations,[191] if one is attached to bliss, one will be reborn in the desire realm of the gods; if one is attached to luminosity, one will be reborn in the form realm of the gods; and if one is attached to conceptionlessness, one will be reborn in the formless realm of the gods. So, these are called deviations.

If this is introduced and explained, what is called bliss means the arising of an experience of joy and bliss that cannot be separated from the natural state of mind, undefiled by the three great root sufferings.[192] It does not mean the arising of the bliss of impure desire, or happiness and pleasure that change through the circumstance of objects.

Clear light means being unadulterated by hindrances such as being enveloped by fogginess or dullness; it is keen awareness or clarity arising unobstructedly. This does not mean the signs of color, shape, and so on, of objective phenomena whose essence is deluded mind's reflections of appearances that come from ego.

Conceptionlessness means being free from diverse conceptions of a solid reality and the turbulent movement of deluded thoughts. It is said that conceptionlessness is like the sky. It is not like the numbness of fainting or the darkness of deep sleep.

In brief, although these three experiences arise spontaneously as signs of the path, aside from that, if one purposely meditates with the hope of having these experiences, grasping at one's meditation as pure and becoming attached to these experiences when they do occur, then this will be the cause of being unable to go beyond the three realms.

As for the four strayings,[193] they are: to stray into emptiness as cognitive knowledge; to stray into emptiness as a path; to stray into emptiness as an antidote; and to stray into an imitation of emptiness. Even though each of them has two types, which are straying from the beginning and temporary straying, if synthesized, the essence of the great emptiness of absolute truth, pure from the beginning, liberated from the ties of fabrication and naming by the intellect, is present awareness, the primordially pure, great directionless expanse. Not understanding this essential meaning, if one tries to achieve emptiness from elsewhere by imposing an imitation that is like emptiness onto phenomena, then this is straying into the nature of substantiality.

Also, if one does not believe in carrying natural, ordinary self-awareness mind to the path, and does not understand that the self-nature of the inseparable basis and result is from the beginning self-accomplished, expecting the Dharmakaya result to occur from elsewhere by effortlessly meditating on an imagined emptiness of the path, then this is straying onto the path.

Whatever passions and conceptions arise, their essence is not other than unsurpassed emptiness from the beginning. So therefore, there is no need either for passions to be abandoned or for emptiness as the antidote. When the abandonable passions themselves are recognized by awareness, they are simultaneously self-liberated, like the knot of a snake releasing itself. Not understanding the essential meaning of this, if one thinks it is necessary to meditate separately on the antidote of emptiness to abandon passions and conceptions, then this is straying to the antidote.[194]

Any meditation practices with or without elaboration are spontaneously perfect from the beginning as the great nondual union of clear light and emptiness in the sky space of great, profound Kuntuzangmo. Not understanding this, if the rigidity of the meditator's mind and his fixation on purifying into aimlessness are not contained in nonduality, it is straying to an imitation of the natural indivisibility of emptiness and awareness. When the meditator is rigid and fixates on purifying everything into aimlessness, this artificial emptiness and mind's awareness do not become nondual, skillful means and wisdom become separate.[195] Without sustaining the continuity of unending natural awareness beyond conception through aimless watchfulness, by keeping previous understanding in mind, if one claims that there is no meditation or meditator, and that all is emptiness, all is Dharmakaya, karmic cause and result are not true but just ideas and conceptions, and nothing ever exists, it is imposing a theory of emptiness as an imitation. There is so much of this these days.

To synthesize, from the achievement by the meditator of the meditation in hand [from the time the meditator knows how to meditate] until the state that is always supreme is reached, there is a very narrow, constricted, dangerous passage with errors, deviations, and strayings. So, if one does not examine these experiences decisively, even if one is expert at using terms and rhetoric, as it is said in *The Great Perfection Tantra*:[196]

Experiences are like mist—they will vanish.

Thus it is said.

Even a small object of good or bad circumstances can lure the meditator because of being lost due to circumstances. So therefore, if one does not have a special method for purifying obstacles and developing experiences, simply doing a strict retreat without meeting people, with tight suppression, boasting, and grasping mind, tying and binding one's posture tightly, visualizing deities and reciting mantra, practicing the meditation of channels and airs and so on, and if one practices these very rigidly, like purposely purchasing hairs of suffering,[197] how is it possible to attain enlightenment?

From *The Sublime Gathering*:[198]

> A Bodhisattva who stays thousands of miles[199] away in
>   the folds of the mountains
> In a place full of snakes, even if he stays there for
>   millions of years,
> Without knowing the true meaning of solitude,
> Develops the arrogance of superiority and remains an
>   ordinary sentient being.

So it is said.

Therefore, by knowing the essential point of carrying whatever arises onto the path, the hermit of one's own mind in the hermitage of one's body dwells in the solitude of practice. Other than that, there is no greater path of approaching enlightenment. So therefore, without the boasts, complaints, and expectations of years or months of retreat, one should dedicate one's entire life, trying to sustain the continuity of uncontrived natural mind. Even whatever good or bad conceptions arise, without thinking they are conceptions, which is putting a patch of naked grasping on them, and without applying the antidote of moxibustion to conceptions as objects to be burned, and so on, just ignore them, like an old man watching the play of children, in the nature that is free from activity. By persisting day and night without interval, the power of conceptionless sublime seeing is perfected. Even

whatever arises such as abiding, movement, mindful awareness, good thoughts, and bad thoughts, one is saved in the
profound Great Perfection, which is great empty awareness
beyond conception.

From *The Great Perfection Tantra*:

Realization is like the sky that never changes.

As for the yogi, even though his body appears to be ordinary,
his mind abides in effortless Dharmakaya wisdom. Therefore, all appearances are the mandala of the sublime Lama,
and whatever arises is all-pervading wisdom. All objects and
appearances are mudra and teaching. Without the effort of
stages or paths, from the expanse of the continuity of enlightened mind in which samsara and enlightenment are primordially liberated, the benefit for the teachings of Buddha and
all sentient beings happens effortlessly and spontaneously in
time. Just as when a vase breaks, the space inside and outside
of the vase become simultaneously inseparable as one taste, so
also, at the time of death, when the trap of the body dissolves,
one is enlightened in the primordial basis of space, the inner
clarity free from examining mind, the youthful vase body.
This is the ultimate accomplishment.

Here, said again:

Relative truth phenomena of delusion, the great lie,
Are swallowed in the great expanse of the nature of
    awareness.
The mind's movement, the activity of a child's dance,

Has vanished in mindfulness beyond thought.
Chasing noble conceptions of the point of view of high
    realization, and
Trapped in doubt by the ties of ignoble conceptions,
Without being intoxicated by the sleep of ignorance
    through drinking this wine,
Abide in ordinary, naked, relaxed awareness mind.
The mouth's point of view, exaggerated through
    pretentious understanding,
And the suffering of being stuck on the narrow path of
    stillness and movement, and so on,
Through the profound speech of the indestructible
    lineage of wisdom,
Are conquered one hundred times by a few verses.
Through the accumulation of the interdependent
    circumstances of previous white prayers,
And by the grace of the union of the profound vajra
    path,
With the handprint of the untying of the central
    channel,
This is made by the experience of the pith of precious
    teachings.
Like that, even though the thunder of the summer
    drum sounding
Bursts the hearts of vain mole[200] scholars,
The profound experience of realization overflows,
So therefore, I could not hide the vast expanse of
    speech.
By this virtue, to sustain the self-nature of mindfulness,
All nonvirtue of a tangled and spoiled mind

Is purified in the spontaneous unending nature.
May all beings realize the Great Perfection.

Chödrung Dampa Longdrol Yingrig,[201] who has the good result of previous fortunate virtue with the wealth of faith, generosity, and having heard many teachings, without ceasing in the practice of the clear light of the Great Perfection, and Kusum Yingrig,[202] who has the disciplined mind of the three solitudes by only abiding in sealed retreat, always practicing the clear light indestructible essence, and others, have not only once but again and again requested this so-named *Lion's Roar: Cutting Through Errors and Deviations*, from one pretending to have the experience of the state of the true nature of the Clear Light Great Perfection, Ku Su Lu'i Naljorpa,[203] Pema Wangchen Yeshe Palgyi Roltsho.[204] This was written in retreat at the Ogmin Khandro'i Tshogkang Sangchen Metok Puk,[205] the assembly hall of the dakini's innermost great secret flower, which is in the center of Glorious Chimphu.[206] Do not show this to those unfortunate disbelievers who did not receive teachings or who, even though they received them, are made crazy by the poisonous water of selfishness without understanding the pith of the path. Those who consider practice to be the essence, read this text seriously. Whoever has inner belief, I have given you the permission and blessing of speech through reading.[207] Most precious heart protectors of Nyingtig,[208] I entrust this to you.

SAMAYA GYA GYA GYA![209]

4 · Always Rejoicing in the Forest

KUNKHYEN LONGCHENPA

I prostrate to my Root Guru and the Triple Gems.

Your forest body, with the peace of fresh flowers
And cool moonbeams of compassion, in flawless joy,
Is the only medicine that refreshes beings who have been
　　tired for so long.
I prostrate to the wonderful forest, which did not exist
　　before.[210]

From the sadness of my mind in the city of existence
Comes this speech of relying on the peaceful grove.
For those who make effort from the heart on the path of
　　Dharma,
This message is spoken by the mind to the mind.

This life is impermanent and will vanish soon.
Even a body that has been cared for so much must be left
And one has to go alone to an unknown place.
Seeing this meaning, now I must go to the forest.[211]

If there is distraction, the path of enlightenment is lost,
Only causing the suffering of samsara to increase.
Seeing this contagion of conception,
I am going to rely on the unborn forest of peace.

In the busy city of the fire pit of desire,
Overpowered by the brutal disease of worldliness,
One wanders again in this abyss of existence.
Seeing this meaning, now I must go to the forest.

Beings of existence, harmed by the passions,
Trapped by the great peril of grasping,
All without exception have been fathers and mothers.
So therefore, to liberate them, I must go to the forest.

Thus, looking toward outer objects,
Everything whatsoever is always impermanent and
     unreliable.
Seeing this movement, like autumn clouds,
From my heart, I must go to the peaceful forest.

The ancient noble suns[212] have set;
The present ignoble moon rises.
Wicked, demonic tribes of darkness pervade in all directions.
Seeing this, now I must go to the forest.

It is extremely difficult to deal with people.
What is good is not admired; what is false is not criticized.
Just for small reasons, so much is expressed.
No matter what is done, there will never be satisfaction.
Now, not staying, I am going to the forest.

If one does not control the mind by one's own mind,
Its direction cannot be changed by others paying attention
     to it.

For the great counsel of my own mind,
Not staying, I definitely am going to the forest.

If one keeps the company of childish people, virtue will be
    obscured.
Some nonvirtue will certainly occur.
So therefore, I myself, only to increase virtue,
From today, definitely am going to the forest.

These days, when spending time together with people,
Instantly friends are made;
Instantly they become untrustworthy like enemies.
Therefore, not staying, I am going to the forest.

Alas, these days, even the teachings of Buddha
Are close to setting at the western mountain peak.
If they set, the sound of the Lion's[213] sacred teachings
Will not occur in the future. I am going to the forest.

If spoken correctly, no one pays attention to the meaning.
If spoken falsely, it is against Holy Dharma.
The Victorious One has said there is no method to please
    him
Other than pleasing sentient beings. Keeping his speech in
    the mind,
keeping his speech in the mind.

If speaking about the path of Dharma, one is abused like an
    enemy by everyone.
If speaking the opposite of Dharma these days,

Sentient beings appreciate it, but it will be the cause of lower
　　realms.
I myself do not understand what to do.
Seeing that meaning, to accomplish benefit for sentient
　　beings,
Not staying, not staying, now I am going to the forest.

Having a tranquil, beautiful body, holding the wings of the
　　three trainings,[214]
Even though a person enters the lotus lake of hearing and
　　contemplating,
When he has no material possessions, he is abused and
　　abandoned by everyone.
The wealthy who have no Dharma and engage in nonvirtue
　　are honored like gods.
The ignorant are valued more than sublime beings.
Seeing this in these degenerate days, I am going to the forest.

Wherever one looks, beings are only exerting themselves for
　　substance.
Effort on the path of Dharma is just like a star in the day.
Seeing this meaning, in order to accomplish the sacred
　　teachings,
Now, not staying, I am going to the forest.

Wherever consideration is given, there is only the endeavor
　　of the busy gathering of passions and karma.
In a hundred paths, practicing according to the way of
　　Dharma is rarely sustained.

Those who practice Dharma in a correct way are ignored
and insulted.
Even for just that reason, I am not staying; I am going to the
forest.

If I look within myself,
This life does not endure through day and night and will
soon vanish.
Virtue is always being destroyed by laziness.
This mind does not stay in stillness even for one moment.
Seeing this meaning, now I am going to the forest.

If praised, then happy; if insulted, then unhappy; and so on.
Distracted by these eight worldly dharmas,[215]
Even though Dharma is being practiced, one is still
overpowered by this life.
Now, not staying, I am going to the forest.

Until yesterday, happiness and entertainment were enjoyed;
Using all these is last night's dream.
Even though remembering them sometimes,
By seeing essencelessness, I am going to the forest.

However many qualities are tasted, there is never
satisfaction.
Since one has been born until now,
However much happiness one has enjoyed,
One is that much more dissatisfied and attached to desirable
qualities again.

In this way, even for this life, there can be no fulfillment of
    happiness.
Wishing to accomplish benefit for many lives,
How can I attain liberation beyond suffering?
Now you have had enough of the path of desire.
You, heart, be inspired from today.
Abandon desire and go to the forest.

No matter how much thought there is, it does not benefit.
So therefore, watch the experience of one's own mind.
From today, in the forest,
You, mind, go to accomplish rejoicing forever.

Sitting in the final bed oneself,
Leaving everything and having to go alone,
Will certainly occur without taking very long.
So right now, go to the forest.

In these extremely defiled times,
Even though someone like me has spoken, there is no benefit
    to others.
I pray it will benefit in future eras.
So therefore, not staying, I am going to meditate in the
    forest.

Since there is no benefit for oneself and no benefit for
    others,
You, mind, forget these aims from today.
To accomplish actual benefit for oneself,
Go to the forest to meditate in the absolute nature of mind.

Later, when the stage of benefit for others is attained,
Without thinking of one's own benefit for even one moment,
To accomplish the benefit of many hundreds of millions of
    others,
I must certainly pray noble prayers from my heart.
If there is presence of mind in the heart,
Do not stay; go to meditate in the forest.

So that one's inferiors should hear and
Especially in order to uphold Lord Buddha's teachings,
Please mainly teach and listen to the essence of teachings.
From that, the teachings of Lord Buddha will flourish and
Wisdom intelligence will increase in one's own mind.
Whatever is thought is impermanent and has no essence.
Even though compounded substances are good, they
    certainly perish.
Seeing this meaning, the essence of the unperishing
    meaning,
Go to find sacred, undeceiving mind.

Whatever possible forms of teachings were spoken by
    Buddha,
All of their meanings are for the purpose of abandoning
    desire
And abiding in the equanimity of the peaceful meaning.
Nothing is spoken by Buddha other than this, so therefore,
    you, mind,
Remember death and definitely go to the forest.

The forest is praised in many ways by the Victorious Ones.
With less desire and more contentment,
These noble beings stayed in the forest.
Now, in this time of unstable conceptions,
It is important to place the mind inward.
In the midst of many people, the mind goes to the object of
    distraction
And cannot stay still even for a moment.
Though the mind is protected well, it follows after the
    passions even so.
Just for those reasons, go to the forest to meditate.

Even though the teachings with characteristics are
    understood, if they are just left to be recalled,
There is no benefit to this.
To experience the qualities of the teachings in the mind,
Do not stay. It is necessary to go to the forest.

The forest has naturally fewer distractions and busy
    gatherings,
And is free from fear and all the suffering of violence.
Happiness there exceeds what is attainable in the city of the
    god realms.
Today, be happy in the tranquil forest.

Hear![216] You, mind, listen to the quality of the forest.
Jewel trees, for worthy offerings to the Victorious Ones,
Are laden with fruits growing pleasantly in the forests,
With fragrant blossoming flowers and leaves.
A cool, aromatic breeze arises with the perfume of incense.

A rocky highland stream gives the melodious sound of a
    drum.
Cool moonbeams pervade the waists of the mountains,
And the clothing of rich, water-holding clouds covers them.

There, completely enhanced by the gatherings of
    constellations,
Flocks of water birds glide over a sweet-smelling lake,
And many kinds of birds and deer wander harmoniously.

Lotus blossoms, wish-fulfilling trees, and blue water lilies
Are surrounded by musical, humming bees.
The swaying dance of young trees and
The fingertips of bowing branches
Seem to welcome guests with greetings.

Cool, pristine water covered with lotuses
Is like the clearly seen complexion of a smiling face.
This natural garden has rosary ornaments of flowers and trees,
And blue grass meadows pleasingly hold the sky-covering.
Stars and planets illuminate the clear heavens
Like gods playing in the garden of enjoyment.

Cuckoos, intoxicated with euphoria, sing beautiful songs.
Flowers are dispersed by the soothing breeze of time
And an elephant of the clouds[217] gives a joyful sound.
The gentle sprinkling of rain is cool, so cool.

Even the food of roots, leaves, and fruits,
Uninfluenced by sin, is in the forest for the four seasons.[218]

Even the passions fade naturally in the forest.
There is no one saying unpleasant words.

Going a long distance from the restless town,
In the forest the samadhi of tranquillity naturally increases.
Complementing Holy Dharma and subduing this mind,
The refined peace of happiness can be attained in the forest.

In brief, the qualities of the forest are unsurpassed,
So how can they be exhausted even if one talks for eons?
Even the Buddhas of the three times attain enlightenment
By remaining in the forest. There is no way other than this.
It does not come by staying in a country or town with
    worldly engagements.[219]

Thus, remembering the qualities of the forest,
If one takes seven steps and turns to a solitary place,
Toward all Buddhas as countless as the sands of the Ganges,
Even the accumulation of the merit of form from offering all
    flowers and incense
Cannot be compared to this.

According to *The Sutra of the Moon Lamp*,[220]
One should think extensively of the precious qualities of the
    forest.
Going there near caves and rock mountains
Or next to valleys of medicine, trees, and flowers,
Make a simple thatched shelter of grass and leaves.
With water, wood, fruit, and so on,

With simple necessities, keep the body living.
Make the virtuous effort of Dharma day and night.

Then, there in the forest, as in the example of old leaves,
The body, youth, and the distinctions of the senses
Gradually, gradually change to essencelessness.
Definitely realize that wealth diminishes.

Then, as in the example of trees and leaves separating,
Those who are friends and those who are not friends and
    also one's body,
Even though gathered together, each has the nature of
    separation.
Definitely realize the nature of separation.

Then, as in the example of an emptied lotus lake,
All various desirable objects and wealth
Are ultimately impermanent, changing, and essenceless.
Definitely realize how all that is collected is exhausted.

Then, as in the example of the changing four seasons,
Even though this body blossoms like an early spring flower,
The aspect of youth vanishes, changed by time.
Definitely realize the Lord of Death will come.

Then, as in the example of ripening and falling fruit,
All those who are old, young, and mature
Have the nature of dying. When it occurs is uncertain.
Definitely realize that to be born is to die.

Then, as in the example of reflections arising in a pool,
All varied phenomena do not naturally exist as they appear.
Like magic, a mirage, and a moon's reflection in water,
Definitely realize they are empty of truth.

Thus, by fully understanding all phenomena,
On an open seat with a straight, relaxed body of ease,
Consider the benefit of all sentient beings and contemplate
    the mind of enlightenment.

Do not think of the past or invoke the future.
Forget thoughts of the present mind.
Do not project and do not absorb. Leave the mind in the
    undistracted state.

Naturally clear, intangibly pristine, sole indivisible light;
Be in empty, clear, nongrasping freedom from elaboration.
This is the wisdom mind of all Buddhas of the three times.

In the unending natural state, the nature of mind as it is,
Abide by freely letting go. Besides that,
Give up thinking of anything.
Without thinking and examining, with no fabricated object,
That is the wisdom mind of the Buddhas.

So therefore, to make peace from the dismal thicket of
    conception,
Watch the absolute state of the profound tranquillity of
    mind.
After that, make the dedication to purify the three circlings.[221]

Between sessions, contemplate the impermanence of death
And the essencelessness of the compounded with so many
    faults,
Which are the nature of samsara. Consider this.

Having realized that all of these various outer phenomena
Are like dreams and magic,
Leave all in the even nature of the sky.
Without accepting or rejecting, let go of thinking about them.
By doing this, whatever appears
Is the unborn and unceasing nature of mind.
The unending nature as it is will occur.

Like this, when going to sleep,
Leave the essential nature of unborn mind
In the state free from the fabrication of perception.

Also, whenever awakening, and when appearances arise,
Watch their nature of nonexistence, like magic, again and
    again.
Whatever appears is the jewel treasure of the essential
    nature of mind.
By seeing the essence of not clearing away and not putting
    back,
And by crossing the ocean of the suffering of existence,
The nonsuffering peace of always rejoicing, the uncontrived,
    sublime continent,
The measureless state of enlightenment, will be attained.

Sometimes, whatever miracles of conception occur,
Watch self-occurrence without grasping, in the essence of
    whatever arises.
The essence of conception becomes the display of
    Dharmakaya.

At the time of going, walking, standing, and seeing,
May I guide all these sentient beings
And thus may I become their protector, refuge, and support.

Definitely dwelling in the thought of enlightened mind
And remembering the way of pure activity,
One should not think of anything other than the benefit of
    all sentient beings.
This is the great tree of compassion
Through which the seedling of the all-knowing Victorious
    Ones flourishes,
Surpassing the Hinayana and Pratyeka states.

The radiance of measureless compassion fully illuminates
The great ocean of inconceivable aspects of infinite qualities.
It is amazing as the jewel of fully enlightened Buddha emerges.
Where is there anything more wonderful than this?

Therefore, those of you who are wise,
In order to accomplish the peace of sacred enlightenment,
Please, definitely go to the forest to meditate.

If Dharma is not practiced in this life,
How will one know where to go in the future?

Then it will be very difficult to meet the path of Dharma.
At that time, nothing can be repaired.
So therefore, right at this moment, great effort should be
made to practice Dharma.

Who knows what certain time, today or tomorrow, death
will come?
The mind cannot be sure; the Lord of Death comes closer
and closer.
One can never turn this back.
Hurry, hurry, please go to the forest to meditate.

Even for someone who has wealth and friends and relatives,
There is no benefit when the time of death comes.
Even though dying, whoever has Dharma has no fear.
Please come here quickly to go together to the forest.

The time when self and others and everything vanishes
Will certainly soon come unhindered.
So, in order to practice Dharma immediately,
Definitely go to the forest.

Those who are ordained and have heard many teachings,
Those who are thorough meditators and remain in the
forest,
Those who have the experience of virtue,
Will fearlessly attain extraordinary joy at the time of death.
The cause of happiness is accomplished by staying in the
forest,
So therefore, please go to the forest to meditate.

Definitely, the time when one no longer exists will come.
Who knows if it will occur even tomorrow, and who has
power over it?
After death, there is no other refuge than Dharma.
Dharma is the refuge and shelter and supporting strength.
Dharma shows the joyful way to the noble house.
So therefore, you, mind, remember death and
Definitely go to the forest to practice.
Please give this message inwardly from the mind to the mind.
If you, mind, listen to this, it is auspicious for Dharma.
Thus this beneficial voice is spoken from the heart.
So you, mind, please go to the forest.

This speech of always rejoicing in the forest,
By the one from the glorious inconceivable place, with a
weary mind wishing for liberation,[222]
Resting on the highest mountain peak of the essential nature
of mind,
Is spoken from the heart for going to the forest.
Whatever virtue is attained from this,
May all sentient beings, wearied by the city of samsara,
In the joyful, omniscient forest of liberation,
Be enlightened simultaneously.

The speech of always rejoicing in the forest was written by
the poet who has heard much, the one from the glorious
inconceivable place with the power of voice,[223] when weary
of samsara on the peak of the highest mountain.

5 · Praise of the Ten Deeds of Buddha

RIGDZIN JIGME LINGPA

From the endlessly joyful city of deathlessness,
The bodhichitta of Sublime White Crown manifested.[224]
The pure vessel holding the sole essence of the Shakya race
Is the doe-eyed Mayadevi;[225]

Like a thousand rays of light shining on the eastern mountain,
The lotus womb blossomed in the garden of Lumbini.
I prostrate to you, worshiped in awe by Brahma and Indra,
The one predicted to attain enlightenment.

Through your prowess in the sixty-four athletic contests,
You defeated young Shakya challengers proud of their
    youthfulness.
By the power of your manifestation, all beings offered
    homage to you, and through your renown
The consciousness of all beings was perfected by seeing and
    hearing you.

Without being conquered by the lasso of ordinary desire,
To please your sole, honorable father,
You watched the magic of the queen from your magic point
    of view.
I prostrate to you, the one who succeeded in ruling your
    kingdom.

Even though worldly kingdoms always change and dissipate
And it is rare for kings not to be lured by a kingdom's hook,
Through weariness from seeing the four great rivers of
    suffering,[226]
You emerged as a self-ordained monk.

By the river Niranjana, in waves of continuous diligence
    without rest,
You endured hardship and subdued thoughts
Through the power of your samadhi.
I prostrate to you, the one who makes all Buddhas of the ten
    directions and four times rejoice.

To make the last of the three immeasurably long eras of
    existent phenomena meaningful,
Bound with the two accumulations,
You annihilated all demonic obstructors of enlightenment
    near the bodhi tree.
You attained enlightenment, the nature of all Buddhas.

Through the ship of the three vehicles, you saved all sentient
    beings
Who were running to the unfathomable, endless precipice of
    samsara,
And guided them to the state of enlightenment.
Buddha, I prostrate to you.

However much wine of intellectual conception anti-
    Buddhists drank,
Just that much was their unruly intoxication.

By cutting their drunken tongues with your miraculous
    truth in the grove of Shravasti,[227]
Their celebrity completely faded in shame.

Because you have attained the four miraculous
    accomplishments,[228]
You have no feeling for birth, old age, illness, or death.
Yet for those who are not concerned with the inevitability of
    impermanence,
You passed into parinirvana to show us the weariness of
    samsara. I prostrate to you.

For unfortunate beings who do not have the accumulation
    of virtue,
To vastly increase the white wealth of Dharma,
You left the unending legacy of eight relics of your wisdom
    body.
You abide in Dharmakaya.

As you have done, may I also purify all obscurations,
Gathering virtue to fully ripen sentient beings to
    Buddhahood.
Enlighten us beyond the three realms to the purest land,
And by ten miraculous deeds, may I benefit sentient beings
    the same as you.

6 · The Treasure of Blessings of the Ritual of Buddha

MIPHAM RINPOCHE

Praise to Guru Shakyamuni.

So, in The King of Samadhi Sutra,[229] *it is said:*

> *Whenever walking, sitting, standing, or sleeping,*
> *For those remembering the moon of Buddha,*
> *Buddha is always there before them,*
> *And they will attain sublime, expansive nirvana.*

And also,

> *Stainless, golden-colored body,*
> *Always exquisite Lord of the Universe,*
> *Whoever beholds this*
> *Is in Bodhisattva's samadhi.*

As it says, our incomparable, victorious Buddha-remembering practice is like this.

I take refuge until I reach enlightenment
In the Buddha, the Dharma, and the Sangha.
I dedicate all my merit, including generosity,
To attain enlightenment for the benefit of all sentient beings.

Thus, refuge and bodhicitta. And:

May all sentient beings be happy.
May they be separated from suffering.
May they never be separated from happiness.
May they realize the equanimity of all phenomena.

These are the four measureless wishes.[230] Having finished these, then, by remembering the point of view that all phenomena appear but do not naturally exist:

Aн
Unborn great emptiness and actual relative truth
Are inseparable, unobstructed, magical appearance.
Before me in the sky, in the center of clouds of offerings
    as vast as the ocean,
On a jewel throne raised by lions, above a lotus, sun,
    and moon,
Is incomparable Lord Buddha Shakyamuni,
Golden-colored with the auspicious signs and noble
    marks,
Clothed in the three robes of the Dharma, sitting in the
    indestructible position,
With right hand extended in the gesture of the earth
    conqueror[231]
And left hand holding a bowl of nectar in the gesture of
    abiding in equanimity,
Glorious and resplendent, radiant like a stainless golden
    mountain.
Patterns of wisdom rays pervade the space of the sky.

The eight Bodhisattvas, the sixteen Arhats, and other
     sublime ones
Are a surrounding ocean of gathered followers.
Just remembering you is release from the two extremes of
     samsara and nirvana.
With the blessing of glorious desireless bliss,
The essence of all Buddhas appears.

Thus, like that, with concentration toward the image of Buddha, Buddha is actually sitting in front of us. The wisdom body of Buddha does not have any partiality of direction or time, so wherever we think of Buddha, Buddha is there.

It is said in the sutras:

> *Whoever imagines Buddha,*
> *Buddha is there,*
> *Always giving blessings,*
> *Liberating from all obscurations.*

Also, whatever virtue is accumulated by focusing on Buddha will be inexhaustible and never wasted.

In the Avatamsaka Sutra, *it is said:*

> *Even hearing, seeing, and offering to Buddhas*
> *Increases measureless amounts of merit.*
> *All suffering of samsaric passions is abandoned.*
> *Virtue will never be exhausted in tangible phenomena.*

For whatever one prays before Buddha, it is fulfilled.

In The Sutra Revealing the Qualities of Manjushri's Pureland,[232] *it is said:*

Since all phenomena come from circumstance,
By completely depending on ultimate intention,
For whatever one prays,
As it is wished, the result is attained.

As it is said, believe this unshakably, and then pray like this:

Taking on the land of misfortune,
You offered five hundred great prayers* through great
    unconditioned compassion.
Praised as a rare stainless white lotus for your exalted qualities,
    just hearing your name is never to return to samsara.

---

*In the previous eon, the most important minister of King Tsibkyi Mukhyu was Gyatsho Dul (Pith of Oceans). His son, Gyatsho Nyingpo (Essence of Oceans), had the thirty-two noble marks and eighty auspicious signs of a Buddha. This son was ordained as a monk, and when he attained enlightenment, he was named Essence of Jewels.

Gyatsho Dul encouraged the king, queens, princes, princesses, ministers, and subjects to take bodhichitta vows from Essence of Jewels to attain enlightenment for the benefit of all beings. The minister himself took bodhichitta vows to benefit all beings, especially the beings of the kaliyuga, and prayed five hundred great prayers before Essence of Jewels. He made offerings of flowers of rejoicing, which he had received from many Buddhafields, to Essence of Jewels, and asked him to predict the Buddhafield in which he would attain enlightenment.

Essence of Jewels said that among the Bodhisattvas, Gyatsho Dul was a supreme Bodhisattva who had prayed for the benefit of the beings of the kaliyuga, so he was as rare as a white lotus among flowers, predicting that he would be enlightened in the Stainless White Lotus Buddhafield of Compassion. Then, referring to our present age, Essence of Jewels predicted that Gyatsho Dul would take the name of Buddha Shakyamuni.

The wondrous previous life histories of Lord Buddha can be read in many sutras, especially the commentary for this *Treasure of Blessings of the Ritual of Buddha*, entitled *White Lotus (Padma Karpo, pad+ma dkar po)*, which tells of these five hundred great prayers, written by the Triumphant One, Victorious in the Ten Directions (Mipham Rinpoche), the emanation of Manjushri.

I prostrate to you, most kind and compassionate Buddha.

The virtue of myself and others, including body, speech, mind, and possessions,

I offer to you in inexhaustible clouds of offering, like Samantabhadra.

From beginningless time until now, the faults and obscurations that were gathered

Are each confessed with regret from the heart without any remaining.

I rejoice in all virtues of ordinary and sublime beings

Accumulated throughout the three times.

I beseech you to turn the profound and expansive wheel of Dharma

Unceasingly toward the ten directions.

Your wisdom body is like the sky,

Living unchangeably throughout the three times.

Even though it is only from our ordinary perception that your body seems to pass away and to be born,

Please always appear in your unobstructed, miraculous emanation form.

May whatever virtue I have accumulated in the three times

Benefit sentient beings as endless as the sky.

May I always fulfill the wisdom mind of Buddha

And may I attain the victorious state of Lord Buddha.

We unfortunate, guideless beings

Are held by your extraordinary, unending kindness.

Whatever pure appearances of the Triple Gems we have in this land and in this time

Only come from your activity.

So therefore, O sole incomparable supreme refuge,

I believe in you with faith and pray to you from my heart.
Without forgetting your previous great promise,
Please hold me with compassion until I reach
    enlightenment.

Then, with strong faith and devotion, concentrating one-point-edly on Buddha as actually sitting before us:

Supreme Guide, the Subduer who has attained enlighten-ment as all Victorious Ones have done, completely perfect Buddha, Glorious Victor, Shakyamuni, I prostrate to you, I offer to you, I take refuge in you.

Recite as much as possible.

For requesting blessings, recite this mantra* from The Essence of the Prajnaparamita[233] *as much as one can:*

TADYATHA OM MUNE MUNE MAHA MUNAYE SVAHA

---

*Buddha Shakyamuni said that the mantra found in this sadhana is the sacred essence of all the Buddhas. Briefly, a simple explanation of the mean-ing of the mantra is:

TADYATHA: "Thus"; a word preceding what is said by Buddha. Buddha is introducing the syllables of the mantra.

OM: The letter of the essence of the wisdom body, speech, and mind of all Buddhas.

MUNE: "Definitely able," as the Victorious One definitely demolishes all obscurations and definitely accomplishes whatever will benefit.

MUNE: Repeating, to stress how definitely Buddha is able.

MAHA: "Great."

MUNAYE: "By this ability."

SVAHA: "May this be established"; calling Buddha to bestow all positive phenomena.

So, directly, the meaning is: Essence of the three wisdoms of all Buddhas, Vic-torious One definitely dispelling all samsaric negativity and definitely guiding to enlightenment, by this great ability, please grant all that is the basis of enlightenment.

One must especially recite the part of the mantra starting with OM. *During these times of recitation, remember the qualities of Buddha. With devotion, focus one-pointedly on the clear wisdom body of Buddha by saying his name and reciting the mantra.*

From Buddha's wisdom body, many-colored wisdom rays greatly illuminate oneself and all sentient beings so that all obscurations are dispelled. The qualities of the path of Mahayana perfectly increase, and the state of never returning to samsara is attained.

In this way, put as much effort into this practice as possible. Between practice sessions, offer mandalas* and praise Buddha with many kinds of prayers. Choosing whatever you wish, such

---

*The four verses of the simple mandala offering are:

> Spreading fragrant nectar and flowers over measureless land,
> Mount Meru and the four continents are decorated with the sun and moon.
> I visualize and offer inconceivable Buddhafields.
> Through this, may all sentient beings abide in pureland.

If we have faith in Buddha, it is necessary to practice according to the aspect of the deity with whom we have a previous karmic connection. Depending on the wishes of each individual, there are many different sadhanas to practice. Everyone has a different idea of the aspect of Buddha. Sometimes Buddha appears in the robes of a monk in order to teach those practitioners who follow the Sutra teachings. Sometimes he appears as Vajradhara wearing a crown and united with his consort to teach those practitioners who follow the Mantrayana teachings. Sometimes, as he predicted in the *Parinirvana Sutra*, he appears as the Lotus-Born to teach those practitioners who follow the Vajrayana teachings, including the Great Perfection teachings. But no matter how he appears, Buddha Shakyamuni is the original source and revealer of the phenomena of all Buddhas, the aspects and forms of all Buddhas, and the teachings of enlightenment of all Buddhas. Of course, there are many sadhanas of Buddha Shakyamuni written by many scholars and sublime beings, but here, to benefit everyone in the degenerate age, I have translated *The Treasure of Blessings of the Ritual of Buddha* written by the Snowlander, Triumphant Ocean, Victorious in All Directions.

as The White Lotus of Compassion Sutra,[234] The Expansive Display Sutra,[235] *the various emanation sutras of Buddha's rebirths,*[236] *and* The One Hundred and Eight Names of the Buddhas Sutra,[237] *read as much as possible. Pray and dedicate the root of all merit that is accumulated to reach enlightenment. Whenever walking, sleeping, or sitting, without forgetting, one must remember Buddha with mindfulness. Especially at night when sleeping, think of Buddha as completely present and alive with his wisdom body radiantly shining in all directions like clear daytime light. Sleep with your perception focused on this, without the interference of ordinary thoughts. Always remember the previous lives of Buddha, the way in which he increased his compassion for other beings, and the histories of all the Bodhisattvas and Buddhas of the three times, in order to turn the mind to follow after their example, to increase unshakable compassion, to use Bodhisattva activity, and especially to practice the meditation of tranquil stillness and sublime seeing. As much as one is able, one should attain the essence of practice. Thus practicing, it becomes meaningful that one has obtained this precious human birth. Many sutras have said that by just hearing the name of our Buddha, one never returns to samsara and is on the path to great enlightenment. From the mantra of Buddha, all Buddhas manifest. Having found this mantra, the King of Shakya was enlightened. Through this mantra, the Bodhisattva activity of Avalokiteshvara became supreme. Just hearing this mantra dispels all karmic obscurations, and vast accumulations of merit are attained without difficulty.*

In The Essence of the Prajnaparamita, *it is said:*

> *By making effort with mantra practice, one will accomplish the object of the practice without obstacles.*

Also, it is said in many other sutras that even if this mantra is recited one time, eighty billion eons of obscurations are purified and one can obtain limitless positive qualities. Buddha said that this mantra is the sacred essence of Buddha himself. It is explained elsewhere how to practice with developing faith, tranquil stillness, and sublime seeing.

This is *The Treasure of Blessings of the Ritual of Buddha.* Won Orgyen Tenzin Norbu,[238] who is a treasure holder of morality, wisdom, and samadhi, requested with auspicious offerings of deities that this ritual prayer be written. Won Rinpoche again requested through Trulpai Ku Jigme Padma Dechen, with superior precious offerings and deities' scarf, that this ritual be completed as soon as possible. So, in this age of degeneration, with unbreakable faith in Buddha, I, Mipham Jamyang Gyatso, one who holds only the name of a follower of Buddha, finished this at Indestructible Treasure Mountain, Perfect Jewel Island, in the Iron Rat Year on the eighth day of the miraculous month. From this, may there be continuous, wondrous benefit to the teachings of Buddha and to sentient beings. May the incomparable blessings of Victorious Buddha enter the hearts of those who see, hear, touch, and remember this.

The wisdom compassion of Buddhas and Bodhisattvas,
Their wisdom activities, wisdom prayers, wisdom
    omniscience, wisdom love, wisdom power,
And whatever immeasurable qualities they have are a
    supreme wisdom miracle.
May all sentient beings become as they are.

[(The prayer above is) also from Mipham Rinpoche.]

OM SU PAR TIK TRA VAJRA YE SVAHA MANGALAM SHU BHAM[239]

7 · The Sadhana of Fully Enlightened Supreme Vajrasattva, Called "The Daily Practice of the Profound Path, Contained in Essence"

KYABJE DUDJOM RINPOCHE

Prostrations to the Guru, Vajrasattva.

For those practitioners who have obtained empowerment in the mandala of Vajrasattva, the essence of all immeasurable Buddha families, and who have faith and keep samaya, this is a daily practice with the yidam, the deity with whom one is indivisible until becoming fully enlightened Buddha Vajrasattva. In order to practice this, there are three categories.

First, the method to connect.

All objects of refuge of the immeasurable Buddhas of all ten directions appear in the aspect of Vajrasattva.

VAJRA SAMADZA

Saying this, visualize Vajrasattva in the sky in front of oneself.

Homage! Vajrasattva, who contains all immeasurable
    Buddha families,
I rely on you inseparably as the supreme refuge.
In order to benefit other beings, for emptying samsara at the
    root,
I will strive to accomplish the profound yoga.

Take refuge and develop bodhichitta three times.

Glorious Buddha, enlightened Vajra Master,
I prostrate to you who always abides throughout all the
    three times.
In you, the Vajra Master who is the Triple Gems,
I take refuge with doubtless faith.
Whatever exists in reality and whatever manifests from mind,
As pure offerings, I offer to you. Please accept them.
I confess whatever negative actions I have done without
    exception,
The obstacles blocking the flow of the river of siddhi.
The pure phenomena that have surpassed the three
    circlings[240] of the ten directions,
I rejoice that they are sustained without attachment.
I develop this complete bodhichitta, [which is]
Naturally stainless with none of the four extremes.
To the enlightened Buddhas and Bodhisattvas,
I offer the forms of the three purities.
The combined virtues accumulated throughout many lives
To the supreme state of enlightenment.

*After accumulating the regular confession of the eight-branch
accumulation, say:*

VAJRA MU

By saying VAJRA MU, *all objects of refuge dissolve into oneself.*

  Instantly visualize oneself as Vajra Heruka and emanate

from one's heart many small wrathful deities with a rain of weapons,[241] exorcising all demons.

Think in this way.

HUNG HUNG HUNG BHI SHO VAJRA KRODA DZO LA
MANDALA PHAT PHAT PHAT HALA HALA HALA HUNG

Thus exorcised.
  Say:

VAJRA JNANA RAKSHA HUNG

Thus, one is protected by an indestructible tent of vajra, padma, kilaya, or chakra, surrounded by a vajra fence.
  If one has set an actual offering, say this:

OM AH HUNG SARWA PUDZA MEGHA SAMAYE HUNG
VAJRA SA PHA RA NA KHAM

Clouds of offerings emanate as vast as the sky.
  Second, the main practice. The yoga of visualizing wisdom body, including its branches:

AH
The display of unborn emptiness, Dharmadhatu,
Is all-pervading, unobstructed compassion.
The self-awareness union of emptiness and clarity
Is the syllable HUNG, white, clear, and radiant.
From that light comes a vajra tent.

Outside of the tent, the display of wisdom fire flames.

Inside, the elements are successively piled.

Above that, in the center of a lotus with a thousand petals
opening,

In the center of a jewel palace with perfectly complete
qualities,

Above a sun and moon, on a lotus and a throne raised by
lions,

From the essence of the syllable HUNG, which becomes a
vajra with a HUNG in the center,

Inconceivable light emanates as offerings to all Buddhas and
purifies all obscurations of sentient beings.[242]

When these lights are gathered back, then instantly

One becomes the wisdom body of Vajrasattva,

Illuminating white light, having the nine aspects of
peacefulness,[243]

With noble marks and auspicious signs, in a flourishing
youthful body,

Wearing a diadem, flowing silken crown scarves, and a blue
silk patterned scarf,

Beautifully adorned with upper and lower garments,

Crown, earrings, and necklace,

Long necklace and jewel rosary,

Ornamented with exquisite bracelets,

Deep blue hair tied up high in a topknot

Adorned with a radiant jewel,

In the right hand, a vajra held at the heart,

In the left hand, a bell held at the waist,

Sitting with both legs crossed in the vajra position.

In his lap is the supreme white consort, Nyema Karmo,

In the youthful aspect of a sixteen-year-old, joyful with
　　wisdom desire,
Adorned with the five ornaments,
With a curved knife in the right hand, embracing her
　　consort,
Offering a skull cup full of nectar in the left hand,
With her legs encircling her consort's waist,
United in great, flawless exaltation.
All energy of the skandhas is the mandala of the wrathful
　　and peaceful victorious ones,
Self-accomplished from the beginning, without searching.
The profound radiating and gathering of immeasurable
　　rays,
The great, all-pervasive origin of all mandalas,
The supreme holder of boundless compassion,
By visualizing the magic emptiness of wisdom body,
With the syllables OM AH HUNG at the three doors,
From the syllable HUNG at the wisdom heart, many lights
　　manifest toward Akanishtha Heaven.
Wisdom Vajrasattva is invoked.

Visualize like that.

OM
From abiding evenly in Dharmadhatu,
All Victorious Ones and Bodhisattvas,
May you arise in the Rupakaya form of Vajrasattva.
I beseech you to come quickly through your compassion.
SAMAYA HO SAMAYA STAM VAJRA SAMADZA JNANA
　　SATTVA AH AH

Thus, request the jnanasattva deity, appearing in perceptible wisdom form from the origin, formless Dharmadhatu, to remain indivisibly with the samayasattva:

DZA HUNG BAM HO
SAMAYA TIKTRA LHEN

Saying this, request the jnanasattva to stay.

Wisdom deities of empowerment fill the sky,
Giving the empowerment of wisdom-amrita.
The five places of the crown are ornamented with the five
    syllables[244]
And the empowerments of the five wisdom Buddha families
    are perfectly complete.

HUNG OM TRAM HRI AH[245]
ABHI KENTSA EMA KO HANG

Thus, the empowerment is given and sealed.

From oneself as Vajrasattva, many offering goddesses
    manifest,
Pleasing with prostrations, offerings, and praise:

AH LA LA HO
ATI PU HO
PRATI TSHA HO

Thus, make prostrations.

OM SHIRI VAJRA RAGA ARGHAM PADHYAM PUSHPE DUPE
ALOKE GENDHE NEWIDYA SHAP DA PRATI TSHA SWA HA

Thus, make outer offerings.

OM RUPA SHAPDA GENDHE RA SA PAR SHE PU DZA HO

Thus, make inner offerings.

MAHA PANTSA AMRITA RAKTA BALINGTA KHAHI

Thus, make secret offerings.

TA NA GA NA DHARMADHATU PUDZA HO

Thus, offer the Dharmata of union and liberation.

HUNG
Indestructible, enlightened wisdom hero, supreme Vajrasattva,
All indestructible, enlightened Buddhas are you.
You are the primordial vajra, Samantabhadra.
I prostrate to you, Vajrasattva.

Thus make offering and praise. Then, all the sky-filling god-
desses are drawn back into oneself.

If one wants to practice in a non-elaborate way as a daily prac-
tice, after the above-mentioned empowerment, one can then go to
the recitation of the mantra. It can be done in that way.

Then, the yoga of the wisdom mantra.

Abiding on the moon in the center of the wisdom heart
Is a five-pointed vajra, in the center of which is

The syllable HUNG, surrounded by the Hundred-Syllable
     Mantra.
From that, boundless light rays emanate.
All the immeasurable victorious Three Roots
Are pleased by the offerings, and all blessings and
     empowerments are received.
Defilements that anger the Dharmapalas are purified.
Fulfilling the solemn oath of their wishes, the
     accomplishment of wisdom activity is requested.
The broken samaya with vajra brothers and sisters
Is cleansed, and complete purity is attained.
The cruel harm of the intentions and negative activities of
     all enemies, devils, and demons
Ceases in peace, and bodhichitta is born.
The cause and result of the suffering of beings in the six realms
Are totally purified, and the completion of the path of
     enlightenment is reached.
The light rays return and dissolve into oneself.
All decayed and broken samaya, sins, and faults are cleansed
     without exception.
The splendor of blessing and great exaltation radiates.
All phenomena of form are the wisdom body of Vajrasattva.
All resonance of sounds is the sound of the One Hundred
     Syllables.
All thoughts are the wisdom mind of Vajrasattva.
The uncontrived, inconceivable pervasiveness of great wisdom
Is all perfectly contained in sole oneness.

Like this, keep the life of sublime wisdom, and then predomi-
nantly recite [the One Hundred Syllables]:

OM VAJRASATTO SAMAYA

MANU PALAYA

VAJRA SATTO TENOPA TICH'TRA

DRIDHRO ME BHAWA

SUTOKAYO ME BHAWA

SUPOKAYO ME BHAWA

ANURAKTO ME BHAWA

SARWA SIDDHIM ME PRAYATSA

SARWA KARMA SUTSA ME

TSITTAM SHRIYAM

KURU HUNG

HA HA HA HA HO

BHAGAWAN SARWA TATHAGATA

VAJRA MAME MUNTSA VAJRI BHAWA

MAHA SAMAYA SATTO AH.

And then:

OM VAJRASATTO HUNG

Thus, also recite the essence of mantra as much as one can.

  Then, if one wants to perform a special practice:

From the rosary of mantra in one's heart,
The light rays of the mantra emanate immeasurably.
Wherever the being is wandering in the six realms,
The light rays of the mantra touch that being.
Negative karma, nonvirtue, and obscurations, including
     their causes, are purified.
Instantly, like awakening from a dream,
The being takes breath in the pureland of Vajrasattva.

The state of constant exaltation is attained.

Again, repeat:

OM VAJRASATTO HUNG
'A AH SHA SA MA HA

Thus, one should recite one hundred, one thousand, ten thousand, or one hundred thousand, according to time or necessity.

Then, when it is time to begin the interval,

OM
O Guru Vajrasattva,
Please protect beings from the worst hells.
I have great remorse for the accumulation of nonvirtues.
Confessing with regret before you, Lord,
I vow never to commit nonvirtue in the future, so
    therefore,
Please completely purify me, Lord.
In order to benefit all beings,
I must accomplish Vajrasattva.
Uniting with the wisdom body, speech, and mind of
    Vajrasattva,
Please guide me to the unsurpassable place.

Thus, by praying, think that Vajrasattva forgives all defilements and all samsaric karma is purified.

Then, the yoga of the great wisdom mind, the sole mandala of the indivisible samayasattva and jnanasattva:[246]

All the outer container of pureland and all the inner essence
 of wisdom Vajrasattva deities melt into light and
 dissolve into oneself,
And oneself dissolves into the heart syllable HUNG.[247]
Then, that syllable HUNG dissolves upward toward the
 nada,[248] vanishing in stainless space,[249]
Limitlessly pervading in profound Dharmadhatu.

*Thus, the phenomena of wisdom deity are gathered into clear
light and then abide in equanimity, the state of Dharmakaya.*

Instantly, from the nature of Dharmata, indivisible
 emptiness and light
Again arise as the wisdom body of Vajrasattva.[250]
The three places are protected by the seal of the three vajra
 syllables.
One enters into beneficial activity for all sentient beings as
 pervasive as the sky.

*Thus, unending wisdom deity arises and all activities are carried
into the display of Dharmata.*
 Now, the third and final category is:

Born in the Vajra family,
Revealing the secret teachings of Vajrasattva,
Having compassion toward beings and faith in my Guru,
May I be born and born in this way until attaining the state
 of Vajrasattva.
Holding the vajra and bell in my hands,

Reading profound upadesha,
Evenly eating the nectar of the wisdom vajra queen,
May I be born and born in this way until attaining the state
    of Vajrasattva.
Whatever merit I have accumulated through this practice
Is dedicated to all limitless sentient beings.
May all attain the supreme state beyond suffering,
The glorious enlightened body of Vajrasattva.

Thus, dedicate virtue and seal pervasively with prayer.

The nature itself is changeless,
The immortal firm essence of Vajra.
In the fathomlessness of the self-awareness wisdom hero,
May the auspiciousness of enlightenment be attained.

*Thus, say these auspicious words, and create happiness and
prosperity.*

Thus, in upper Tibet, around Ladakh, by the request of
Unchanging Vajra of Dharmadhatu,[251] who is always raising the banner of retreat, this is composed by gathering
many essences from the tantras, transmissions, and upadesha of Vajrasattva from the teachings of the lineages of
Vajradhara and terma, by the wanderer in all countries,
Fearless Wisdom Vajra, Jigdral Yeshe Dorje. May it be beneficial for all beings.

SARWA DA MANGALAM

Ritual to Accompany the Vajrasattva Sadhana for Beings Who Have Passed Away

[*The following text by Kyabje Dudjom Rinpoche includes a brief introduction and some comments by Kyabje Thinley Norbu Rinpoche. The recitation is in roman type, and any italicized words in brackets are comments by Kyabje Thinley Norbu Rinpoche (not for recitation).*]

In Buddhism, there are many different traditions of what is done for the dead, such as reading sutras, especially the Prajnaparamita. The traditions of inner Vajrayana include differences in what is done when an ordinary being passes away and when a sublime being passes away. All of these traditions can be known from many texts, sadhanas, and their commentaries, in a brief, informal way or in an elaborate way, which have to be studied or learned from a highly realized wisdom teacher. In order to benefit beings of this degenerate time to keep them from falling into nihilist ideas, and at least to benefit dying and dead beings to keep their bodies from just being thrown out in an ordinary way to get rid of them, without considering the continuity of mind until attaining enlightenment or how to support their next lives, this sadhana has been included here.

According to different religious ideas, there are different ways of understanding the elements and what should be done with corpses in relation to the elements, so many people follow what they consider to be the best way according to their tradition. Here, I will explain in a brief way about the elements in relation to corpses according to the Buddhist tantric Vajrayana tradition. Of course, for whoever has realized this according to the high inner tantric tradition, all elements are pure manifestations of the Five Wisdom Consorts, so there is no discrimination between the elements, which are equally pure. But according to ordinary relative truth, earth is heavier than water, water is heavier than air, air is more substantial than fire, and the lightest element is sky. So sometimes the corpse of someone who has died of some terrible disease that can be contagious to others and cannot be burned has to be buried in the earth far away from others for months or years until the corpse has vanished into the earth and left only a skeleton so as not to spread disease. Other than that, if there is no terrible disease, a corpse can be thrown into the water of a clean, strong river with prayers and the intention of benefiting and feeding water beings. Then, normally, for ordinary beings, the best way is to burn the corpse, because the lightest element according to relative truth is the sky, and it is the fastest method, symbolizing that there is no residue of ordinary samsaric phenomena remaining.

Instructions about the dead have been consolidated here in the simplest way because all of the world is changing. Countries are changing, and towns are changing into cities, which in general are governed by many nihilist laws that require corpses to be buried or burned as soon as possible and do not allow them to be kept for seven or twenty-one or forty-nine days according to traditions for ordinary dead people. Even when corpses are burned, there is no chance to burn them in a traditional way according to the ritual of a fire puja with many necessities and substances, including medicinal herbs, oils, and piled wood, as well as synchronized mantras and prayers. Sometimes there is no time for these rituals because corpses are cremated by putting them into an electric stove, instantly burning them. The Vajrayana always has so many different methods corresponding to the capacity of beings and adapting to time and place. So here, according to these conditions, without contradiction between what is traditional and what is nontraditional, I am trying to show what can be done in the simplest way without being against the laws of modern countries, and how with good intention, Buddhist rituals can be done according to the phenomena, tradition, and satisfaction of Buddhists.

First, there are two different categories of rituals. One category is not done with the actual corpse. This ritual can be done for someone who has passed away, even though, through circumstances, there is no actual corpse present.

Without creating anything that is in front of oneself, such as visualizing oneself and then again visualizing another mandala in front of oneself, so that one is here and another is there, visualize oneself as Vajrasattva according to the sadhana in the mandala of Vajrasattva. Then, write the name of the person who passed away and the syllable ཉྰ [NI], which symbolizes the consciousness of that being, on a piece of paper. Put this paper on a stick and place the stick on an eight-petaled lotus. This [name inscription for the deceased] is called a mingjang.[252]

The substances of sand and sesame seeds are used for the purification of obscurations and for exorcising whatever connection the being may have with any negative influence. Also, foods should be set in front of the mingjang, including whatever foods the being liked when he was living. Personal belongings of the being who has passed away, such as medicines, papers, Dharma texts, and even suitcases can be put in front of the mingjang in order for it to be recognized by the being.

Then, one first says the Seven-Line Prayer to Guru Rinpoche three times. After that, the sadhana of Vajrasattva can be started *and continued up to the mantra, counting the elaborate mantra and after that counting the brief essence mantra.*

Then, after saying:

'A AH SHA SA MA HA,

say:

AH SU NI TRI PRE DU

These are the seed syllables of the six realms.

SARWA PA PAM KLESHA DA HA NA BHASMI KU RU SO HA

One has to recite this and then blow on the sand and sesame in order to use it later to scatter for purification and exorcism of the mingjang.

Then say:

OM SUMBHANI SUMBHANI HUNG
GIR HANA GIR HANA HUNG
GIR HANA PAYA GIR HANA PAYA HUNG
A NAYA HO
BHAGAWAN BIDAYA RAZA KRODHA HUNG PHAT

With these words, the mingjang is cleansed. Then, with these words:

OM SO BHAWA SHUDDHA SARWA DHARMA SO BHAWA
SHUDDHO HANG,

it is cleansed into stainless emptiness. From emptiness, in emptiness, visualize that the mingjang, the syllable NI on a lotus seat, becomes the actual dead person. Then pray to the Triple Gems, and especially Vajrasattva, who is the essence of all immeasurable Buddhas.

Namo! Homage to the Triple Gems. By the power of the truthful words of the Triple Gems, [especially Vajrasattva, who is the essence of the power of all immeasurable Buddhas,] and by the truth of extremely pure Dharmata and the infallibility of the cause and result of relative truth, and the truthful words of the assembly of yidam deities of the mandala, by the blessing of this great truth, the being who passed away, called [the name of the being] instantly comes from wherever he is wandering in any of the three realms and four ways of taking rebirth to this mingjang, [which becomes real and the same as living.]

OM BENZAR AH KAR KAYA DZA

This mantra draws the consciousness of the deceased being.

SARWA PA PAM ANAYA HUNG

This mantra gathers all the nonvirtues of the deceased being. Visualize while saying:

DZA HUNG BAM HO

The aspect of consciousness becomes a white AH and dissolves into the mingjang. [With these words, the being comes with his habits and the aspect of his consciousness.]

For purifying obstacles, visualizing oneself as Vajrasattva:

From the wisdom heart of oneself as Vajrasattva come many wrathful deities who exorcise whoever is harming the dead being.

HUNG HUNG HUNG
BISHO VAJRA KRODA DZO LA MANDALA PHAT PHAT
    PHAT
HA LA HA LA HA LA HUNG

Thus, exorcise with this mantra.
   Then, for the purification of nonvirtue:

Visualizing oneself as Vajrasattva, with hands held together, visualize the five fingers of the right hand as the five male wisdom consorts, and the five fingers of the left hand as the five female wisdom consorts.

Then clasp one's hands for the union of the male and female deities. Then say:

HUNG OM SO ANG HA,

the syllables of the five male consorts, and:

MUM LAM MAM PAM TAM,

the syllables of the five wisdom Dakinis. Then visualize the five male and female wisdom consorts in union and say:

OM SU RA TA TAM

Clasp the fingers of the hands together and say:

VAJRA ANZALI

Then say:

VAJRA BHANDHA BAM

while squeezing the hands and fingers together. Then the male and female consorts of the five Buddha families are united.
Then say the Hundred-Syllable Mantra of Vajrasattva:

OM BENZAR SATTO SAMAYA
MANU PALAYA BENZAR SATTO
TENOPA TICH'TRA DRIDHRO ME BHAWA
SU TO KAYO ME BHAWA
SU PO KAYO ME BHAWA
ANU RAKTO ME BHAWA
SARWA SIDDHIM ME PRAYATSA
SARWA KARMA SUTSA ME
TSITTAM SHRIYAM KURU HUNG
HA HA HA HA HO
BHAGAWAN SARWA TATHAGATA
BENZAR MAME MUNTSA
BENZRI BHAWA
MAHA SAMAYA SATTO
AH

After that, say:

VAJRA BHANDHA TRA TA SARWA PAH BAM PRAVE SHAYA
PHAT

and release the gesture of the hands. Think that: The light of
the five Buddha families emanates like sun rays toward the
mingjang. The light touches the form of that being, and all
obscurations are purified.

*Also, for purification, say the Hundred-Syllable Mantra, and
then say the following mantra three or seven times, scattering
the sand and sesame seeds that were previously blown on with
mantras.*

OM DA HA DA HA SARWA NA RA KA GATE HETUN HUNG
     PHAT
OM PATSA PATSA SARWA PRE TA KA GATE HETUN HUNG
     PHAT
OM MATA MATA SARWA TRI YA KA GATE HETUN HUNG
     PHAT

Visualize while saying:

All obscurations, without leaving any residue, are extremely
purified like dew that has melted into dryness by sunshine.

*In order to purify the cause of the six realms, including their
habits, visualize and say:*

The essence of that being's habit of the six realms of many
lives until now becomes the white letter AH [*the syllable of the
habit of the god realm*] on his forehead; the blue letter SU [*the
syllable of the habit of the asura "realm"*] on his neck; the green

letter NI [*the syllable of the habit of human beings*] on his heart; the yellow THRI [*the syllable of the habit of the hungry ghost realm*] at his secret place; and the black letter DU [*the syllable of the habit of the hell realm*] under his feet.

Also, the white syllable OM, the seed of wisdom body that inherently exists, is on the forehead of the form of the being. The red syllable AH, the seed of wisdom speech that inherently exists, is on the throat of the form of the being. The blue syllable HUNG, the seed of wisdom mind that inherently exists, is on the heart of the form of the being. These syllables are very clean, sparkling, and radiant. Then, from the wisdom heart of oneself visualized as Vajrasattva, many lights emanate and strike the syllables on the form of the being. From the connection of these radiant lights landing on and dissolving into these syllables, by the flaming of wisdom fire, all the syllables of the six realms, including all residue, are totally burned without leaving even an iota of anything.

Then say 108 times:

OM AH HUNG

It is necessary to recite these three vajra wisdom syllables. Then:

The essence of the being becomes the white letter HUNG, and the HUNG is transformed into the body of Vajrasattva.

Then, in order to give empowerment:

From the heart of oneself visualized as Vajrasattva, many lights emanate, and the Buddhas and Bodhisattvas of all ten directions, including the five Buddha families united with wisdom consorts, manifest in front of the samayasattva of this being. The five Buddha families and consorts are invited onto the crown chakra of the being. They unite, and from this exaltation, the consorts melt into the wisdom nectar of flawless exaltation and flow on the five places of the head of the being.

Then say:

HUNG OM SO ANG HA ABHISHEKA ATMA KO HANG

Then empowerment is received. All five passions are purified, and the five skandhas of the being are transformed into the five Buddha families. Then the nectar of the initiation ascends again and goes up on the crown of the being and is sustained there, becoming the crown of the five Buddha families.

Then scatter flowers, saying:

OM SUPRA TIKTHRA VAJRA YE SO HA

In order to give food offerings to the dead being and train him on the path, arrange whatever food and drinks in front [of the mingjang], and cleanse and purify them with the syllables:

RAM YAM KHAM

Visualize while saying:

The five desirable qualities, including beautiful form, pleasing sound, delicious taste, perfumed smell, and smooth touch, fill the sky in an immeasurable way.

Then say this blessing three, five, or seven times:

NAMA SARWA TATHAGATE BHAYO BISHO MUKHE BHAY
SARWA T'HA KHAM UT GATE SAP'HARANA IMAM GAGANA
KHAM SO HA

To you who have passed away,
Beautiful form, sound, smell,
Delicious flavor, smooth touch, and so on,
I offer you the five desirable qualities to delight you.
Enjoy these excellent sense objects
And be satisfied without attachment.
May you accomplish wisdom bliss.

Then think that the dead person has received the offering.
The object to whom the offering is made is the mandala of
Vajrasattva. The object that is offered is immeasurable qualities.
The one who is offering has pure intention. The three purities are
offered to the mandala of Vajrasattva, saying this:

The body, speech, and mind of the Buddhas of the three times
Are the wrathful and peaceful mandala of Vajrasattva.
I offer all immeasurable offerings with my body, speech, and
    mind.
May you liberate all three realms in unborn Dharmakaya,

The nature pure from the beginning.
By the activity of the union of merit and wisdom,
Please guide beings who are wandering in the in-between state
Toward enlightenment with the hook of compassion.

Having prayed in this way, say:

From the wisdom heart of oneself abiding in the phenomena of Vajrasattva, boundless rays of compassion emanate in the form of hooks to the being who has passed away. The being's sole essence of wisdom is transformed into stainless wisdom with the aspect of a letter HUNG, pulled through the being's crown chakra, guided, and ejected to Akanishtha Heaven, dissolving into the heart of Vajrasattva.

Thinking like that, the mingjang is burned with the flaming light of a butter lamp, saying:

HUNG
In the fireplace of Dharmadhatu,
The fuel of grasping is burned by wisdom fire.
The passions of the being who has passed away are burned
      without leaving even a trace.
According to absolute truth,
What is burned and those who burn
Have no existence and are from the beginning enlightened.
So, self-accomplished Dharmakaya
Effortlessly opens by self-appearing stainless wisdom.

Saying the Hundred-Syllable Mantra, burn the mingjang.

Saying:

AG NE ZO LA RAM,

think that the five skandhas are completely transformed into flaw-less immortal wisdom body.

Then, dedicate the merit like this:

Just as a lotus is not obscured by mud,
So that person is never affected by the dust of the three
    realms,
Born like a blossoming lotus in pureland.
May the being who has died be born in the pureland of
    Amitabha.

Then, from the fire's leftover ashes, one is supposed to make small tsa-tsa, which are small stupas. In order to make these, on the ashes, visualize this way:

On a moon with a stainless letter AH, many white rays beam, and then from those rays, so much wisdom nectar continuously flows. All obscurations and all samsaric residue are cleansed without an iota remaining.

Then say the Hundred-Syllable Mantra many times, blowing on water and clay to mix with the ashes to make the small stupas. When the tsa-tsa are made with clay, the clay has to be visualized as a pile of jewels. When making the stupa, from the bottom, put the Hundred-Syllable Mantra or the briefer Six-Syllable Mantra inside, written in saffron ink. If for some reason this could not be done due to circumstances, then blow mantra on rice or any pure grain and put this inside. Then, when the stupa is made, think that Rupakaya arises from Dharmakaya and say:

OM SUPRA TIKTHRA VAJRA YE SO HA

8 · The Rain of Blessings

Guru Yoga in Connection with the Seven-Line Prayer

MIPHAM RINPOCHE

Here is the Seven-Line Prayer to Guru Rinpoche.

HUNG! In the northwest of the land of Oddiyana,
At the essence of lotuses,
The wondrous, supreme accomplishment has been attained.
Renowned as the Lotus-Born,
Surrounded by a retinue of many wisdom Dakinis,
Following you to be like you,
I beseech you to come and bless me.
GURU PADMA SIDDHI HUNG

·   ·   ·

Kuntuzangmo, the stainless space of appearance, the consort
    from whom all Buddhas are born,
Sole mother who protects all Tibetan subjects with great
    kindness,
Queen of the great exaltation wisdom Dakinis who bestows
    the supreme attainment,
Yeshe Tsogyal, I pray at your feet.
Please pacify all outer, inner, and secret obstacles.
Please give blessings that the life of the Lama be firm.

Please grant blessings to pacify all times of illness, famine, and war.
Give blessings to pacify all defilements, black magic, and curses.
Give blessings to increase life, glory, and knowledge.
Give blessings for all wishes to be spontaneously fulfilled.

> This prayer to Yeshe Tsogyal was written by the son nursed by wisdom Dakinis, Khakhyab Dorje.[253] May it increase auspiciousness.

AH

In my ordinary body, before me in the sky
Is the stainless lake Dhanakosha of Oddiyana,
Deep and full of water with the qualities of the eight branches.[254]
In its center is a stalk with a fully bloomed jewel lotus.
Upon this is the source containing all refuges, Orgyen Dorje Chang,[255] Vajra Holder of Oddiyana,
With the all-illuminating glory of the signs and marks of the Buddhas, in union with the consort Yeshe Tsogyal.
Holding a vajra in the right hand and a skull cup containing a vessel of nectar in the left,
Beautifully adorned with silks, jewels, and bone ornaments,
Magnificent great bliss radiates from the profound space of the five lights.[256]
Surrounded by the ocean of the Three Roots[257] gathered like clouds,
Raining compassion and blessings, please watch over me.

To the deathless wisdom body, essence of all victorious
      Buddhas,
With longing and strong faith, I prostrate to you always.
My body, possessions, and accumulation of virtue in the
      three times
I offer visualized as the clouds of offerings of Kuntuzangpo.
I confess all sins and faults without exception accumulated
      from beginninglessness until now.
In the qualities of all the victorious Buddhas with their
      heirs,
In the history of the sole pervasive Lord,
I rejoice from the heart and pray with faith.
I request a great rainfall of profound, expansive Dharma.
With all the virtue that exists of myself and others combined,
As long as the ocean of realms of sentient beings remains,
I follow your sublime history, supreme guardian,
And dedicate the virtue for the purpose of guiding beings as
      pervasive as the sky.
Great treasure of omniscient compassion, the source
      containing all refuges,
Precious supreme refuge for this degenerate time,
Tormented by pain from the five defilements,[258]
With great longing, I pray that you will think of me, your
      child, from your compassionate heart.
Reveal the unobstructed skillful means of great kindness
      from your profound wisdom omniscience.
Please grant blessings to my devoted heart.
I beseech you to show signs and indications quickly,
And to bestow general and supreme accomplishments.

HUNG! In the northwest of the land of Oddiyana,
At the essence of lotuses,
The wondrous, supreme accomplishment has been attained.
Renowned as the Lotus-Born,
Surrounded by a retinue of many wisdom Dakinis,
Following you to be like you,
I beseech you to come and bless me.
GURU PADMA SIDDHI HUNG

Recite the Seven-Line Prayer as many times as possible. After that, recite the Vajra Guru mantra. By the devotion of prayer, wisdom light rays of five colors are extended in lines from the place of wisdom union and the wisdom heart of the joined male and female consorts, and dissolve into one's heart, bestowing blessings. If one wants to end the practice with light initiation after the recitation of mantra, all sublime retinues, including the Three Roots, dissolve into Guru Rinpoche and his consort. Both consorts dissolve into oneself, and one becomes the same as they are, as explained later. If one wants to make tsok offerings in daily practice, and particularly on special days such as the Tenth Day, one should offer according to this Tsok of the Glorious Pure Vessel after the recitation of mantra, before taking light initiation and dissolving. Arrange pure substances, including wine and meat with which one has not been involved in harming the being's life, and then pray and offer according to the meaning of the following verses.

HUNG
From AH, a skull cup as limitless as Dharmadhatu;
From OM, all existent phenomena are arranged as
    measureless desirable qualities of tsok;

By HUNG, it is transformed into the display of great bliss
    wisdom nectar;
By HRIH, the gathering of deities of the Three Roots is
    pleased and fulfilled.
OM AH HUNG HRIH
This blesses the tsok.

Then, invoking the object of refuge and making offerings.

HUNG! In the northwest of the land of Oddiyana,
At the essence of lotuses,
The wondrous, supreme accomplishment has been attained.
Renowned as the Lotus-Born,
Surrounded by a retinue of many wisdom Dakinis,
Following you to be like you,
As I invite you to these desirable tsok offerings,
I beseech you to come and give blessings.
Please consecrate this supreme place and bestow your
    blessings.
Transform the offerings into wisdom nectar.
Bestow the four empowerments on me, a devoted
    practitioner of the supreme way.
Dispel demons, reversed guides, and obstacles.
Bestow supreme and general accomplishments.

HUNG
Supreme lotus Lama who wears a rosary of bone ornaments,
With a gathering of Dakinis and Vidyadharas,
The mandala of the victorious Buddhas containing all Three
    Roots

I pray to you with strong longing devotion.

My own and others' three doors, of body, speech, and mind
including accumulated virtue and wealth,

And the desirable qualities of whatever phenomena exist
without any imperfection,

I offer as the unending gatherings of great bliss of
Kuntuzangpo.

Please accept these offerings with joy, and may your
unconditioned wishes be fulfilled.

I pray to you, Guru Rinpoche.

Bestow blessings, Vidyadharas and Dakinis.

Grant supreme and general accomplishments to your son,
a devoted follower.

Purify all broken and faded samaya.

Liberate all outer, inner, and secret obstacles into wisdom
space.

Hold me inseparably until I attain enlightenment.

Increase my life, merit, spiritual experience, and realization
like the waxing moon.

Bless me so that all my aspirations are effortlessly fulfilled.

OM AH HUNG VAJRA GURU PADMA SIDDHI HUNG

*Now, the recitation of the brief tsok offering. Bless the substances
with:*

OM AH HUNG HO

Gathering of deities of the Three Roots, come to the tsok
offering.

I offer the outer, inner, and secret offerings of great bliss.

I humbly confess all broken samaya.

Annihilate and free the enemy of duality and obstructions in
    Dharmadhatu.
May the bliss of great equanimity fulfill your unconditioned
    wishes.
I pray that you bestow supreme and general
    accomplishments.

*This short tsok was also written by Mipham Jampel Dorje, so
it can be used for the accumulation of tsok.*

Song of Delight and Satisfaction

All beings are the manifest nature of supreme joy.
The yogini is the naturally dwelling mandala.
All beings of the three realms without exception are natural
    Buddhas.
Together with them, transformed through compassion into
    youthful Dakinis, we enjoy these offerings.
Alas, ignorant cattle do not understand this.
Beautiful, inherent Dakinis accept it in great bliss.
Whoever does not meditate in absolute truth
Will not attain Buddhahood.
Understand that inner and outer are indistinguishable
And thus you will be able to annihilate all worldliness.
Alas, ignorant cattle do not understand this.
Beautiful, inherent Dakinis accept it in great bliss.

OM AH HUNG
Wild, worldly spirits who eat the remainder of the offerings
Gather like clouds and eat ravenously.

Devour the remaining offerings of meat and blood.
As you have promised before,
Devour the enemies of Dharma and those who break their
    vows.
Show us signs and indications quickly.
Dispel obstacles to accomplishment
And perform activities beneficial to Buddha's teachings
    unobstructedly.

UTZIGTA BA LING TA KHA HI

Saying this, put out the remaining offerings.
    At the end of the session of practice:

From the three syllables[259] in the Lama's three centers,
White, red, and blue light rays emerge,
Dissolving into my three centers so the obscurations of my
    three doors are purified
And transformed into wisdom vajra body, wisdom vajra
    speech, and wisdom vajra mind.
Finally, the Lama and his retinue dissolve into light,
And a red and white sphere marked with HUNG
Is absorbed into my heart. The Lama's wisdom mind
And my mind abide inseparably in spontaneously born
    Dharmakaya.

A AH

Saying this, watch one's own natural mind that is beyond
acceptance and rejection, from the beginning uncontrived, and
primordially the self-face of great Dharmakaya. Again, see all
magical phenomena as naturally the Lama, and then dedicate the

merit for all sentient beings, including oneself, to attain enlighten-
ment, which is the state of Padmasambhava and the essence of all
Buddhas, saying auspicious words and expanding propitiousness.

> On the eighth day of the waxing moon of the Drozhin month called "training all beings," I, Mipham Namgyal, wrote this from the lake of my mind, praying to follow Guru Padmasambhava throughout all of my lives.
>
> SARWA MANGALAM

9 · The Assembly Palace of Great Flawless Exaltation, Radiant Lotus Light

KYABJE DUDJOM RINPOCHE

HRI! In the assembly palace of great flawless exaltation,
　　Radiant Lotus Light,
Maha yogis and yoginis are accomplishing the great flawless
　　wisdom exaltation,
Offering sublime, great flawless exaltation amrita,
Illuminating clouds of wondrous, great flawless exaltation.
Great flawless exaltation queen, Yeshe Tsogyal, and your
　　gathering of Dakinis,
May I fulfill your great flawless exaltation wisdom
　　Dharmakaya mind.
All-pervading lord, essence of all Buddha families, holder of
　　unchangeable boundless light,
Buddha Amitabha, may I fulfill your unconditioned wishes.
Subduer of all beings by the treasure of your compassion,
Avalokiteshvara, may I fulfill your unconditioned wishes.
Conqueror of all samsara and nirvana who wears a rosary of
　　bone ornaments,
Supreme victorious vajra dancer, Padmasambhava, may I
　　fulfill your unconditioned wisdom heart.
Supreme principle of the mandala, abiding in Dharmakaya,
Victorious Ocean of Wisdom, Yeshe Tsogyal, may I fulfill
　　your unconditioned wishes.

Those who subdue by any skillful means according to
    sentient beings' phenomena with miraculous activities,
All one hundred thousand Dakinis, may I fulfill your
    unconditioned wishes.
Holders of unobstructed miraculous activity,
Keepers of pure samaya, Dharmapalas, may I fulfill your
    unconditioned wishes.
Whatever samaya of the Vajrayana tradition
Is broken, I confess.
Please purify outer, inner, and secret obstacles
In inconceivable, flawless wisdom light.
May all supreme and common siddhis
And activities be accomplished in this life.

Translated with my daughter, Pema Chökyi, Happy Lotus
of Dharma, just before the tenth day of the Tibetan sixth
month, according to the terma tradition, the great birthday
of Lotus-Born Padmasambhava. [Kyabje Thinley Norbu
Rinpoche]

10 · Calling the Lama

KYABJE DUDJOM RINPOCHE

In the center of the thousand petals of the heart,
In the center of the lotus essence,
Always giving blessing,
Always being with me inseparably in joyfulness,
Supreme Master, glorious Heruka,
Fearless wisdom vajra,
You are the essence of all Victorious Ones.
Believing from the heart with total trust,
With intense yearning,
Praying to you one-pointedly,
By the amrita of the siddhi of empowerment and blessing,
May you please ripen my mind and liberate me.
From remembering my Guru so very much,
Fervently calling with desperation,
Besides this unending nature of my mind, I could not find
    my Guru somewhere else.
The object of praying
And the one who prays, if they do not exist,
With contrived intention, supposedly praying
With effort and grasping: why is it necessary to pretend like
    this?
Unrecognizable clarity,
The naked, raw nature of empty awareness,
This is the only absolute Guru.

I recognize this is Yeshe Dorje.
It is the great abiding nature from the beginning.
In the primordial basis,
There is no need to call from far away,
There is no need to search nearby.
In the all-containing nature beyond thought,
Of course, there is not even the name of delusion,
So therefore, without question, it is enlightenment.
Great, even, inconceivable exaltation,
Whatever arises is all the display of Dharmakaya.
The great blessing, which is free from any aim,
I, a yogi, absorb in my heart.
O great wondrous awe.

For auspiciousness, I translated this from the speech of my Guru Vajradhara Jigdral Yeshe Dorje. [Kyabje Thinley Norbu Rinpoche]

11 · The Guru Yoga of Receiving Wish-Fulfilling Great Flawless Exaltation

KYABJE DUDJOM RINPOCHE

Prostrations to the holy Root Guru.

Definitely believing the most kind Root Guru is great Vajradhara and praying to him are the unmistaken essence of the path of Vajrayana. So therefore, whoever wishes can make effort in that way, encouraged by the weariness of samsara and uncontrived faith.

AH

I take refuge in the absolute self-awareness Guru
Who is never gathering or separating.
I develop bodhichitta in the great self-sustaining nature
Containing all phenomena, the inconceivable Mahasandhi.

Thus, take refuge and develop bodhichitta.

AH

The unobstructed, nonfabricated nature
Is actually seeing the great pureland of Dharmata,
The evenly open clear light of pervasive space,
The increasing, immeasurable palace of the experience of
    pure phenomena.
In the center of the joyful, self-accomplished array

Is the perfect culmination of the complete awareness Guru.
From the miraculous wisdom beyond thought, the
    exhaustion of phenomena,
The great transformation of the youthful vessel body arises.
Yeshe Dorje Heruka[260]
Is the color of a radiant ruby, indivisible exaltation and
    emptiness,
With the face of sole awareness, always smiling in the zenith
    of ecstasy,
And two hands, the union of the actual two truths,
Holding a vajra, conquering samsara and nirvana,
And a kilaya weapon,[261] completely annihilating the
    conception of ego.
Legs are extending in the gesture beyond samsara and
    nirvana,
Crushing the male and female rudras of dualistic
    phenomena.
Demonstrating the adornment of never abandoning all
    desirable qualities,
Wearing the hero's tiger skin around his waist
And bone and jewel ornaments,
He embraces the self-luminous wisdom Dakini in his lap,
Totally naked, holding a curved knife and a kapala of
    rakta.[262]
Both are in enchanting, youthful great exaltation.
From the beginning, self-manifesting and self-occurring,
The spontaneous nature accomplished from the beginning
    appears without visualizing.

Thus, see this.

To the Dharmakaya Root Guru, self-abiding in the original
purity of the basis of Dharmakaya,
I prostrate by recognizing.[263]
I offer the unsought, self-occurring offering,[264]
The self-accomplished, unobstructed phenomena of the
basis.[265]
I confess the deluded obscurations of temporary conceptions
In great, primordially cleansed emptiness.
I rejoice in unmade, even pervasiveness,
The great, vast self-liberation of samsara and nirvana.
I request the turning of the wheel of the empty resonance of
Dharma[266]
By the sounding of undestroyable, clearest, nonsubstantial
speechlessness.
I pray to stay in the great rainbow body,
The profound great transformation of the youthful vessel.
I dedicate the unending, self-sustaining gathering of great
merit
In Dharmadhatu, free from effort and activity.

Thus, accumulate with the seven-branch supplication.[267]

Changeless, unceasing wisdom, the quality of purity from
the beginning,
By coalescing with the youthful, indestructible union of
great exaltation,
Is the one who binds all existence in the depth of the
inconceivable ecstasy of impenetrable oneness.
To my self-awareness Root Guru, Samantabhadra, the
unconditioned state,

Free from the aim of conceptualizing, I pray.
Liberated from the shell of the meditation of contrived
    thoughts,
The natural self-condition of never having meditated,
By the experience of confidence in samadhi, is leaving purity
    as it is without doing anything.
All the residue of samsaric phenomena is exhausted
    inwardly in stainless space.
May you only give the blessing of liberation in that
    self-Dharmata.

*Thus, by one-pointedly praying when experiencing devotion and
faith:*

Lights emanate from the three vajra doors
Of the glorious Guru Heruka.
By dissolving into one's three doors,
All empowerments of wisdom body, speech, and mind are
    received.
The unbearable, flawless exaltation energy of the male and
    female wisdom consorts
Intensely flames, and then melts into a sphere of light,
Dissolving into one's sole, indestructible heart center.
The great empowerment of the blessing of transmission is
    obtained.
In the inconceivable expanse of wisdom mind, realization
    and liberation are simultaneous,
Abiding in awareness of primordial purity, the greatest
    perfection.

Thus, abide in the state of even stillness, freed from all elaboration of thought, as much as you can. Then, when thoughts arise, see all phenomena, sound, and thoughts as the wisdom body, wisdom speech, and wisdom mind of the Root Guru, and then enter into Dharma activity.

Thus, due to the request of one who has the wealth of devotion and samaya, Gelong Tamding Tshewang, who holds the life of Hayagriva, who asked for a Guru Yoga with precious upadesha, this is written by Jigdral Yeshe Dorje. Always auspicious. [This colophon was written by Kyabje Dudjom Rinpoche. The colophon below was added by Kyabje Thinley Norbu Rinpoche.]

Due to Lama Tsedrup Tharchin asking me many years ago to write my own Guru Yoga, I translated this precious Guru Yoga full of the meaning of Dzogpa Chenpo into English as a substitute for writing one myself. May it benefit the lucky students of this degenerate time who have deep devotion and faith in the teacher who reveals the point of view of Dzogpa Chenpo, such as the representative of Samantabhadra, Jigdral Yeshe Dorje, to attain enlightenment.

Notes

Praise to Longchenpa

1. rgyan drug mchog gnyis. The Six Ornaments are Aryadeva, Vasubandhu, Gunaprabha, Sakyaprabha, Dignaga, and Dharmakirti. The Two Excellences are Nagarjuna and Asanga.

2. This does not mean keeping both samsara and nirvana in the forest. This means the complete perfection of the purification of samsara and nirvana.

Praise to Jigme Lingpa

3. gling pa, or Islander. In this case, the word *island* does not mean only an island in this world, but a totally different universe independent of and separated from others, extremely isolated from other lands or the material world. This is not the same use of the word *ling* that refers to the continents of this world, as in the Abhidharma tradition. Here, it is immeasurable mandala, different than other beings' phenomena. *Pa* is a particle indicating ownership or one who resides in a place; here it is like the *–er* in *Islander*.

Praise to the Melodious Wisdom Goddess Saraswati

4. A lake-born flower is an epithet for a lotus (mtsho skyes).

5. This refers to Kunkhyen Longchenpa. Samyepa Mangdu Tho-pa'i Nyen Ngag Khen (bsam yas pa mang du thos pa'i snyan dngags mkhan) is Kunkhyen Longchenpa referring to himself as a poet who has studied and listened extensively to teachings, joining this with his epithet: the One from the Inconceivable Place (Samyepa, bsam yas pa).

6. Lhundrup Ri Rinchen Jungne (lhun grub ri rin chen 'byung gnas).

Praise to Patrul Rinpoche

7. The Victorious Ones are Buddhas, and a Son of the Victorious Ones is a Bodhisattva.

8. One of the eighty-four mahasiddhas.

9. sdug bsngal rang grol, "Self-Liberation of Suffering," an epithet of Avalokiteshvara.

10. Another name for Patrul Rinpoche.

1. The Practice of the View, Meditation, and Action, Called "The Sublime Heart Jewel"

11. Buddha Shakyamuni was worshiped and praised by eternalist gods such as Indra, Brahma, nagas, and many other gods, and that is why Buddha Shakyamuni is called the supreme god of gods.

12. (1) The power of support: power created using an image of sublime beings in a tangible or intangible form. (2) The power of regret: obscurations are dispelled through the power of weariness and regret. (3) The power of the antidote: merit is accumulated through the power of applying antidotes. (4) The power of never returning or of restoring pure wisdom energy: purity is attained, resulting in confidence.

13. The vase empowerment (bum pa'i dbang), secret empowerment (gsang ba'i dbang), prajna-jnana empowerment (shes rab ye shes kyi dbang), and precious word empowerment (tshig dbang rin po che).

14. Deity reliant mantras, obtaining accomplishment mantras, and activity mantras are mantras with different concentrations and aims.

15. The two obscurations of passion and cognition.

16. The four activities are peaceful activities (pacifying obscurations), increasing activities (increasing benefits), magnetizing activities (bringing conditions under power), and wrathful activities (subduing evil and unfavorable interrupting forces).

17. Tsa-tsa are miniature clay stupas or deity images, generally made from molds and usually placed in large quantities in stupas or stored in housing specifically for tsa-tsa.

18. The seven periods are intervals within the seven weeks following death, during which rituals are performed for the deceased, particularly at weekly intervals starting from the date of death and continuing every seventh day for seven weeks.

19. In Tibetan, *bu thang* means mag pa, a bridegroom who stays in his wife's family house, considered an undesirable situation.

20. Namkhai Gyalpo (nam mkha'i rgyal po).

21. Donyö Shagpa (don yod zhags pa).

22. Khorwa Dongtrug ('kor ba dong sprugs).

23. Drodul Thugje Chenpo ('gro 'dul thugs rje chen po).

24. The eight consciousnesses are those of sight, sound, smell, taste, touch, consciousness, passions, and the basic consciousness of not being and not not being, yet also not Dharmakaya.

25. Gyalwa Gyatsho (rgyal ba rgya mtsho).

26. kha sar p'a Ni.

27. Seng-ge Dra (seng ge sgra).

28. Semnyi Ngalso (sems nyid ngal gso).

29. Jigten Wangchug ('jig rten dbang phyug).

30. The wisdom lineage of Kunkhyen Longchenpa and Rigdzin Jigme Lingpa.

31. Desire, hatred, ignorance, pride, and jealousy.

2. Mindfulness, the Ocean of Qualities

32. Dzogpa Chenpo (rdzogs pa chen po), the Great Perfection. *Dzogchen* is an abbreviated form of the term *Dzogpa Chenpo*.

33. rang byung rdo rje, Self-manifesting Indestructibility. One of the names of Kunkhyen Jigme Lingpa (kun mkhyen 'jigs med gling pa). Although this entire text is considered to have been written by Rigdzin Jigme Lingpa, the first four paragraphs are written in the third person, in contrast to the rest of the text, which is a first-person narrative.

34. Chiwa Mepe Jong ('chi ba med pa'i ljong) in South Tibet.

35. mon ljongs mkhar.

36. Rigdzin Jigme Kundrol (dge slong bla ma, rig 'dzin 'jigs med kun grol) is requesting teachings from Rigdzin Jigme Lingpa.

37. U-Tsang: dbus and gtsang.

38. Kama, bka' ma. The original speech of Vajradhara, an aspect of Samantabhadra, which was revealed by Vajrapani, an emanation of Vajradhara.

39. Terma (gter ma) are secret, precious hidden treasures, sealed by manifestations of Vajradhara such as Padmasambhava and many other sublime wisdom saints, to be revealed at the right time for the benefit of sentient beings in the degenerate age. They emanate in the form of teachings and various objects, and are concealed within any of the five elements or within the minds of treasure revealers, tertöns (gter ston).

40. bka' brgyad. The eight sections of the mandala of the sadhanas of Manjushri, Wisdom Body of All Buddhas ('jam dpal sku); Wisdom Speech of the Lotus Buddha Family Lineage (pad ma gsung); Completely Enlightened Wisdom Heart (yang dak thugs); Nectar Qualities of the Buddhas (bdud rtsi yon

tan); Aspect of the Activity of All Buddhas (phur ba phrin las); All Existent Worship ('jig rten mchod bstod); Annihilating Wrathful Mantra (dmod pa drag sngags); and Guru Who Is the Lineage Holder of the Vidyadharas (bla ma rig 'dzin).

41. *byang chub sems dpa'i sde snod;* Skt. Bodhisattvapitaka.

42. Kunkhyen Jigme Lingpa.

43. *theg mchog mdzod.* Part of *The Seven Treasures* of Gyalwa Longchenpa.

44. rgyal ba (Gyalwa) klong chen pa.

45. *Gelong* (dge slong) means "monk," referring to Gelong Lama. This is the beginning of the reply by Kunkhyen Jigme Lingpa, which is the main teaching.

46. Gönpo Ludrup (mgon po klu sgrub).

47. The ten nonvirtuous actions (mi gewa chu, mi dge ba bcu) are the three of the body, which are killing (srog gchod pa), stealing (ma 'byin pa len pa), and adultery ('dod pa'i log gyem); the four of speech, which are lying (rdzun), slandering (phra ma), using harsh words (tshig rtsub), and gossiping (ngag 'khyal); and the three of mind, which are covetousness (brnab sems), mental harm (gnod sems), and having a reverse point of view (log lta), such as disbelieving in the Triple Gems, karma, and so on, according to Buddhist doctrine. The ten virtuous actions (gewa chu, dge ba bcu) are the abandonment of the ten nonvirtues.

48. *mdo sde yon tan bkod pa.*

49. Buddha is described as resembling precious land. Just as land sustains all life as the source of all plants and crops that grow from it and nourish beings, Buddha sustains all beings as the source of blessings that can open the qualities of enlightenment through accumulation for whoever connects to him.

50. chu smad.

51. pha dam pa, "Sacred Father." Phadampa Sangye, an eleventh-century Indian Master, also known as Naljor Dampa (rnal 'byor dam pa), came to Western Tibet and introduced the Shije tradition, the pacification of all suffering, which is one of the eight major spiritual traditions of Tibet.

52. dge slong dri med 'od. Monk of Stainless Light.

53. *sor phreng gi mdo.* Skt. *Angulimala Sutra.*

54. Nonvirtue.

55. Virtue.

56. tekpa sum, theg pa gsum, "three yanas." In general, according to Sutra, the three vehicles are the Shravakayana, Pratyekayana, and Mahayana, but in this case, the Shravaka and Pratyeka are included in the Hinayana as one vehicle, the Yogachara and Madhyamaka are included in the Mahayana as one

vehicle, and all Vajrayana is one vehicle. According to the New School Tantra tradition, the mother tantra, father tantra, and nondual tantra are included in Vajrayana. According to the Nyingma tradition, Mahayoga, Anuyoga, and Atiyoga are included in the Vajrayana.

57. theg pa gsum gyi rten. The vows of the three vehicles are sdom pa, Hinayana vows; bslab bya, that which has to be learned, Mahayana vows; and dam tshig, Vajrayana vows.

58. rigs can gsum. The three faculties of Hinayana, Mahayana, and Vajrayana.

59. The Hinayana, Mahayana, and Vajrayana vows.

60. blo gros rab gsal gyis zhus pa'i mdo.

61. The twelve qualities of practice (sbyangs pa'i yon tan bcu gnyis) are: depending only on alms, staying on one mat while eating, and not eating more than one serving of food; wearing only the three Dharma clothes, sitting on an animal skin, and wearing clothes from corpses in graveyards; staying in a quiet and isolated place, under a tree, without a roof, and in a charnel ground; and sitting steadily upright, in one position without changing it.

62. Jowoje (jo bo rje, 982–1054).

63. The abandonment of samsara and the realization of wisdom mind.

64. brtul zhugs. In general, according to practitioners, brtul means ending previous thoughts, and zhugs means entering a new way of seeing that elevates the practitioner to a higher state of realization. In this case, however, regarding the quality of Buddha, brtul means subduing whatever is necessary, and zhugs means manifesting whatever is necessary for the benefit of guiding sentient beings, according to their faculties, on the path of enlightenment, with unobstructed illumination.

65. After accepting an arrow-maker's daughter as his consort.

66. The vows of pratimoksha, Bodhisattva, and sacred mantra.

67. A bird with a special melodious song.

68. The six extremes (mtha' drug) are (1) drang don, relative meaning, which is whatever belongs to ordinary phenomena that are born, cease, and remain, and whatever is expressible, and how these can be used in teachings of the path of enlightenment; (2) nges don, absolute meaning, which is free from being born, ceasing, and remaining, and whatever is inexpressible, such as the nature of sky wisdom mind, and explanations of teachings of this to attain the result of enlightenment; (3) dgongs pa, the meaning according to Buddha's omniscience, which is seeing the true nature of equanimity, seeing throughout time from timeless wisdom mind for the benefit of beings, seeing for the purpose of other beings although Buddha's mind is unconditioned enlightenment, and seeing what others cannot see, such as beings that exist in other

realms of existence; (4) ldem dgongs, the meaning according to seeing what to reflect to other beings with skillful means in order to guide them onto the path, which are the skillful means of characteristics, the skillful means of antidotes, and the skillful means of transformation; (5) sgra ji bshin pa, the meaning exactly according to the words; and (6) sgra ji bshin ma yin pa, the meaning not according to the words.

69. The four methods (tshul bzhi): (1) The meaning of terms. This is whatever a teaching explains, such as philosophical explanations according to the Sutra tradition, explanations of the four kayas according to the Mantrayana tradition, or explanations of the chakras according to the tantras. (2) The general meaning of teachings. Whoever is attached to a lower yana and afraid of a higher yana, such as Mantrayana, needs an explanation. This general explanation is given, since if one has fear of a high point of view and unusual, extraordinary activity, and is not released from impurity and purity, then one cannot see the meaning of equanimity. If one has a good motivation, however, then one can transform seemingly nonvirtuous activity and cause virtue, even according to the Sutra tradition, or one can use the Mantrayana tradition while keeping one's activity in accord with the Sutra's aspect of the path. (3) The hidden, inconceivable meaning of teachings of the higher yanas. Teachings such as those on the visualization and completion stages and those on Dakinis must be practiced and explained secretly. (4) The ultimate meaning. The teaching of the inseparable two truths and clear light itself or the highest point of view of the highest teachings.

70. grub mtha' gsum, the three doctrines of the Hinayana, Mahayana, and Vajrayana.

71. spyod' jugs.

72. byang chub sems dpa'i sde snod; Skt. Bodhisattvapitaka.

73. Drangsong Zopar Mawa (drang srong bzod par smra ba), Patient Sage. Skt. Kshantivadin. A prior incarnation of the Buddha.

74. thabs la mkhas pa'i mdo sde.

75. gzugs bzang mo.

76. kun dga' bo, All Joy. Lord Buddha's cousin and closest disciple.

77. mnyan yod.

78. licchavi dri med grags pa. Skt. Licchavi Vimalakirti. Licchavi means "of a noble family of Magadha" in Vaishali.

79. rin chen spungs pa.

80. mon pa is a general name for the people of the Himalayan border region between Tibet, Bhutan, Sikkim, Nepal, Burma, and India, including the area of Pemakö. Here, a tribal monpa woman is given as an example of a simple

teacher, and the coral she is wearing is given as an example of Dharma teachings. This refers to those who are only interested in receiving Dharma teachings from their teacher without acknowledging the teacher's qualities.

81. *dren pa nye bar bzhag pa'i mdo.*

82. rgyal po mya ngan med. Buddhist emperor of India, reigned 268–232 B.C.E.

83. mes dbon rnam gsum. The ancient Tibetan Dharma kings Songsten Gampo (srong btsan sgam po), the manifestation of Avalokiteshvara; Trisong Detsen (khri srong lde'u btsan), the manifestation of Manjushri; and Tri Ralpachan (khri ral pa can), the manifestation of Vajrapani.

84. The four activities of daily life are eating, sleeping, going, and staying.

85. The three faults of the container are (1) not listening well with a focused mind, but being like an upside-down pot; (2) even though listening, still not registering in one's heart what is heard, like a pot with a hole in the bottom that cannot hold any essence; and (3) even though listening and registering what is heard, not having the intention of the ultimate benefit of attaining enlightenment, but having the poisons of ego, such as the intention of building one's reputation, like a pot with poison in it.

86. The six stains are (1) arrogance, such as thinking that one is more learned than one's teacher; (2) not having faith in Lamas and Dharma; (3) not being interested in making effort in a pure way; (4) being too susceptible to distraction by outer phenomena; (5) having too much tension because of rigidity and inward suppression of the senses; and (6) listening, but without the weariness of samsara, so that if teachings last a long time, one is tired, unhappy, and bored.

87. The five faults of not retaining the meaning are (1) focusing on the words, but not paying attention to the meaning; (2) focusing on the meaning, but not paying attention to the words; (3) paying attention, but misinterpreting the meaning of the words; (4) focusing, but with disorder; and (5) focusing, but registering the reverse of the meaning.

88. *dkon mchog sprin.*

89. Ösung ('od srungs), Protector of Light. A disciple of the Buddha.

90. Sacred promises.

91. *spyod pa'i sa.*

92. shi-ne (zhi gnas). Skt. shamatha.

93. The four worldly meditations are thought, analysis, joy, and bliss.

94. The four formless equanimities are (1) limitless sky, when phenomena cease to appear; (2) limitless consciousness, when inner insight is attained and outer phenomena do not appear; (3) nothingness, when feelings are as in

a deep sleep; and (4) existence and nonexistence, when neither existence nor nonexistence is experienced.

95. There are different explanations of cessation, including the cessation of all gross passions.

96. lhakthong, lhag mthong. Skt. vipashyana.

97. The five sciences are art, medicine, literature, philosophy, and the meaning of inner awareness.

98. rngog lo chen po, the Great Scholar and Translator of Ngog.

99. has po ri. A hill near Samye Monastery. Padmasambhava summoned supernatural beings there, where they were subdued and bound by samaya to protect Buddha's Dharma.

100. 'jam dpal rtsa rgyud.

101. mnyam gzhag.

102. man ngag rin po che'i mdzod.

103. Effortless mindfulness.

104. Mindfulness with effort.

105. rnam par thar pa. For those who read Tibetan, be careful here; this term seems to be used in a positive way, but its meaning is "faults."

106. rdo rje yang thog rgyud.

107. The perfection of wisdom, or sixth paramita.

108. chönyi (chos nyid); Skt. Dharmata.

109. Gomrim (sgom rim) by Kamalashila.

110. Tibet.

111. dbu ma rang rgyud pa. Skt. Svatantrika-Madhyamaka.

112. The idea is that the Uma Thalgyurpa (Skt. Prasangikas) disproved and surpassed the Uma Rang-gyupa (Skt. Svatantrikas).

113. dbu ma thal 'gyur pa. Skt. Prasangika-Madhyamaka.

114. Chigchar Jugpa (cig car 'jug pa).

115. sems med pa'i gnas skabs lnga. The five mindless states are the cessation of nothingness, perceptionlessness, deep sleep, the total intoxication of no-mind from the effect of alcohol or drugs, and fainting.

116. dbus mtha', one of the Five Treatises of Maitreya.

117. 'od gsal.

118. stobs bcu. According to Mahayana tradition, all of the immeasurable qualities of Buddhas are contained within the qualities of Dharmakaya and the qualities of Rupakaya. The qualities of Dharmakaya are the result of freedom. Among these qualities, one of the many categories is the ten powers: (1)

gnas dang gnas ma yin pa mkhyen pa'i stobs: the power of knowing beings' faculties and what is and is not suitable for them. (2) las kyi rnam par smin pa mkhyen pa'i stobs: the power of knowing the exact causes and results of beings' karma. (3) mos pa sna tshogs mkhyen pa'i stobs: the power of knowing the different wishes of beings. (4) khams sna tshogs mkhyen pa'i stobs: the power of knowing the energy and senses of beings. (5) dbang po mchog dman mkhyen pa'i stobs: the power of knowing the inferior and superior faculties of beings. (6) thams chad du 'gro ba'i lam mkhyen pa'i stobs: the power of knowing the way of going on all the different paths of enlightenment. (7) kun nas nyon mongs pa rnam par byang ba mkhyen pa'i stobs: the power of knowing beings who have purified the passions. (8) sngon gyi gnas rjes su dran pa mkhyen pa'i stobs: the power of remembering former places, without premeditating. (9) 'chi 'pho ba dang skye ba mkhyen pa'i stobs: the power of knowing the transformation of the next life and where that being will be born. (10) zag pa zad pa mkhyen pa'i stobs: the power of knowing those whose passions have been exhausted and who have reached the stage of enlightenment. The qualities of Rupakaya include the thirty-two noble marks and eighty auspicious signs.

119. *stong phrag brgya pa* (The Prajnaparamita in One Hundred Thousand Stanzas).

120. rab 'byor, a disciple of the Buddha. Skt. Subhuti.

121. de bzhin gshegs pa. Skt. Tathagata.

122. That is, according to the tradition of the Bodhisattvayana.

123. The four stages of the path are the path of accumulation, the path of joining, the path of seeing the true nature, and the path of meditation.

124. mi slob lam. The path of no more learning, which is the state of Buddhahood.

125. In the system of the ten bhumis, the eleventh bhumi is Buddhahood, corresponding to mi slob lam, the fifth stage of no more learning.

126. 'od gsal chen po'i dbang. Empowerment received by tenth-stage Bodhisattvas. Following that empowerment, they attain enlightenment.

127. sems sde.

128. klong sde.

129. man ngag sde.

130. be ro tsa na.

131. gnyags (Jnanakumara of Nyag).

132. I.e., from the time of Guru Rinpoche's disciples, in the eighth century.

133. nyang shes rab 'byung gnas, Occurrence of the Source of Wisdom.

134. Siddhi is spiritual accomplishment; supreme siddhi is enlightenment.

135. mi pham mgon po, Triumphant Lord.

136. ngan lam byang chub rgyal mtshan, Sign of Victory of Unobscured Enlightened Attainment.

137. za dam rin chen dbyig, Essence of Jewels.

138. khu 'gyur gsal, Clarity of Release from Decrease.

139. nyang byang chub grags, Renowned Unobscured Enlightened Attainment.

140. dbu ru zha'i nyang shes rab 'byung gnas, Occurrence of the Source of Wisdom from Uru Sha.

141. skor ye shes bla ma.

142. zur chung shes rab grags pa.

143. khams, the region known in English as Eastern Tibet or East Tibet.

144. a ro ye shes 'byung gnas, Occurrence of the Source of Beginningless Wisdom.

145. klong thang sgron ma, Light of the Profound Plain.

146. *thek chen rnal 'byor.*

147. kha rag sgom chung, Little Meditator from Kharag.

148. gcog ro.

149. ya zi.

150. rong zom pan dit.

151. bla ma zur dzongs pa gsal.

152. rgyal rong brag, Victorious Rock Mountain.

153. gyu sgra snying po, Essence of Turquoise Sound.

154. rgyal ba [conqueror] klong chen rab 'byams, one of the names of Longchenpa.

155. The Mind Section, the Expanse Section, and the Precious Teachings Section.

156. thod rgyal.

157. ka dag.

158. lhun grub.

159. khregs chod.

160. la bzla'i grub mtha'.

161. nam par thar pa'i sgo gsum. The three doors of liberation are the door of great shunyata, the door of noncharacteristics, and the door of nonwishing.

162. *Tsalchen; rtsal chen.*

163. *de bzhin gshegs pa'i snying po*. Skt. *Tathagatagarbha Sutra*.

164. *rgyan stug po bkod pa*. Skt. *Gandavyuha Sutra*.

165. *myang 'das*.

166. *sam bhu ti*.

167. *dgyes pa rdo rje*, Laughing Vajra.

168. *sdom 'byung*, Origin of Vows.

169. *bshad rgyud rdo rje phreng ba*, Vajra Mala Tantric Commentary.

170. *lan kar gshegs pa*.

171. The pure nature is the uncontrived essential nature of Dharmata.

172. *dge slong mon pa*, Gelong from Mon.

173. *la stod chos rje*.

174. Chökyi Dragpa (*chos kyi grags pa*).

175. *spa gro kun grol*.

176. *khams pa dge slong*.

177. The path of enlightenment.

178. *gling sras mgon dbang*.

3. The Lion's Roar

179. *rgyud sde*.

180. *mgo ma bskor ba*. This literally translates as "the head cannot be turned," which means here that one cannot be deceived by indifferent stupor.

181. The Lama.

182. The disciple.

183. *mnyam gzhag*.

184. The demon son of the gods is one of the four demons: the demons of the passions, the son of the gods, the skandhas, and death. "Being very attached to desirable qualities causes the demon of the son of the gods, which causes beings to suffer by being lured" (*A Cascading Waterfall of Nectar*, p. 92, n. 133).

185. The speaker, Rigdzin Jigme Lingpa, explains that it is hopeless for whoever speaks like this, because no one is going to understand or listen. Therefore, he is as rare as a white crow.

186. With mind, one can even put a bone in one's heart, which shows the strength of diligence.

187. *rjes thob*, "after attaining nonduality."

188. The four extremes are existence, non-existence, both existence and non-existence, and neither existence nor non-existence.

189. spros pa'i mtha' brgyad. The eight extremes of elaborations of the partiality of views are: not ceasing ('gag pa med pa), not being born (skye ba med pa), not coming ('ong ba med pa), not going ('gro ba med pa), not eternalism (rtag par lta ba ma yin pa), not nihilism (chad par lta ba ma yin pa), not different (mtha' dad ma yin pa), and not the same (don gcig ma yin pa).

190. Even though the text says "da lta'i shes pa," it does not mean the ordinary consciousness of the six or eight consciousnesses, because it is awareness mind beyond conceptualization.

191. gol sa gsum.

192. sdug bsngal gsum. The three great sufferings are the suffering of change, as momentary happiness suddenly changes to suffering; the suffering of suffering, as before previous suffering is finished, new suffering is added to it; and the suffering of gathering, as although it is not recognized, even what is not apparent suffering is the cause of suffering.

193. shor sa bzhi.

194. The conceptions and passions that are to be abandoned are recognized by awareness. When passions and conceptions arise, there is no need for an antidote to purify them, because they are self-liberated since they are unsurpassed emptiness.

195. This reference to aimlessness is not actual emptiness. If the indivisibility of awareness mind and emptiness is realized, it is itself Kuntuzangmo. But if this is not understood and one grasps at aimlessness, so that one is trying to do something with oneself as a meditator who is trying to make emptiness, then actual emptiness and skillful means are going to separate.

196. rdzogs chen rgyud.

197. This is an example of how, without realization and a correct point of view, each small, subtle action is as futile as trying to find tiny hairs. That the hairs are being bought means that this is not natural. Instead of paying attention to what is natural and recognizing the correct point of view, they are searching and shopping for each minute hair, which is an example of the small, rigid ideas that cause fabrication.

198. 'phags pa sdud pa.

199. The text says, "five hundred yojana." A yojana (Tib. dpag tshad) is an ancient Indian measurement of distance approximately equal to 4.5 miles.

200. A reference to the subterranean animal.

201. chos drung dam pa klong grol dbyings rig.

202. sku gsum dbyings rig.

203. ku su lu'i rnal 'byor pa.

204. pad ma dbang chen ye shes dpal gyi rol mtsho.

205. 'og min mkha' 'gro'i tshogs khang gsang chen me tog phug.

206. mchims phu.

207. lung.

208. snying tig.

209. Sometimes placed at the end of a terma to indicate its special nature or secrecy.

4. Always Rejoicing in the Forest

210. In these four lines of praise, the forest is a metaphor for the body of the Root Guru and the Triple Gems, which are inseparable. The rare and inconceivable qualities of the Triple Gems are hidden from nonspiritual beings and do not appear to ordinary, obscured phenomena. In Tibetan poetry, this metaphorical style is called gzugs can gyi rgyan.

211. When Longchenpa speaks about himself, this meaning should not be misinterpreted. He has given himself as an example, but he has actually done this in order to teach other beings.

212. "Noble suns" refers to sublime beings and pure Dharma traditions.

213. The Lion is a metaphor for Buddha Shakyamuni, who is supreme among beings.

214. The three trainings (bstab gsum) are morality (tshul khrims), meditation (ting nge 'dzin), and wisdom (shes rab).

215. The eight worldly dharmas are to like being praised, to dislike being insulted, to like being happy, to dislike being unhappy, to like having a good reputation, to dislike having a bad reputation, to like obtaining material wealth, and to dislike not obtaining material wealth.

216. kye ma, an exclamation of calling.

217. The sound of gentle thunder.

218. These foods are not connected with the mental actions of human beings, so they are not connected with sin. They grow naturally without human intention or interference, so there are no chemicals used and they are not cultivated in any way that would involve killing sentient beings.

219. 'du 'dzi, the amassing of passions and karma that cause turbulent, bustling worldly engagement.

220. *zla ba sgron me'i mdo.*

221. Any virtue that is made, such as praying, giving, offering, visualizing, or meditating, always automatically contains the three circlings. In prayer, the three circlings are the one who prays, the prayer itself, and the object to

whom one prays. When dedicating the merit of virtue, one must abide in sole, stainless mind so that these three circlings become purified because there is no object or subject, which is the cause of the state of Dharmakaya, ultimate enlightenment.

222. The glorious inconceivable place is Samye (bsam yas). "The one from the glorious inconceivable place" is Samyepa (bsam yas pa), an epithet of Kunkhyen Longchenpa.

223. "Glorious Inconceivable One with the Power of Voice" (Palden Samyepa Ngag gi Wangpo, dpal ldan bsam yas pa ngag gi dbang po) is an epithet of Kunkhyen Longchenpa.

5. Praise of the Ten Deeds of Buddha

224. Dampa Togkar; dam pa tog dkar. Skt. Shvetaketu. A Bodhisattva who was born in Tushita Heaven as a son of a god, who would become Buddha Shakyamuni in his next life.

225. Goddess of Magical Emanation; mother of the Buddha.

226. The four great rivers of suffering are birth, aging, sickness, and death.

227. The ancient city of India called Nyenyö (mnyan yod) in Tibetan.

228. According to the *Nitartha International Online Dictionary* (http://www.nitartha.org), the four great miracles are contemplation, consecration, empowerment, and offering.

6. The Treasure of Blessings of the Ritual of Buddha

229. *ting nge 'dzin rgyal po'i mdo.*

230. The four measureless wishes are love, compassion, rejoicing, and equanimity.

231. The "earth witness" mudra.

232. *'jam dpal zhing gi yon tan bstan pa'i mdo.*

233. *sher phyin yi ge nyung ngu.*

234. *snying rje pad dkar*

235. Gyache Rolpa, *rgya che rol pa.*

236. *skyes rabs* (also known as the Jataka tales).

237. *de bzhin gshegs pa'i mtshan brgya rtsa brgyad pa.*

238. o rgyan bstan 'dzin nor bu, 1851–1900.

239. This concluding mantra is not for recitation, but for auspiciousness.

7. The Sadhana of Fully Enlightened Supreme Vajrasattva, Called "The Daily Practice of the Profound Path, Contained in Essence"

240. 'khor gsum. There are many categories of three circlings, but in this case, the three circlings are the subject, the object, and the way they function together. These three circlings are the root cause of samsara, which is purified by sole awareness mind, free from the conception of the three circlings.

241. These weapons, such as sharpened wheels, phurbas, curved knives, and swords, are not tangible, real weapons but aspects of wisdom that destroy duality.

242. Inconceivable light is offered to all Buddhas, and the light returns to the vajra and immeasurable blessings are received. The light again emanates to the six realms of beings, purifying the obscurations of all beings.

243. These are the nine signs of wisdom body of the peaceful Sambhogakaya deities. A pliant body is the sign that ignorance has been purified. A well-toned body is the sign that desire has been purified. A delicate body is the sign that pride has been purified. A perfectly proportioned body is the sign that anger or hatred has been purified. A youthful appearance of the body is the sign that jealousy has been purified. A clear body is the sign that the defect of stains has been purified. A radiant body is the sign of containing all excellent qualities. An attractive body is the sign of having the perfection of all the thirty-two noble marks and eighty excellent signs together. Splendor and blessing of the body are the signs of vanquishing everything.

244. The five places are the center of the forehead, above the tip of each ear, the crown aperture, and the back of the head opposite the center of the forehead.

245. HUNG is the seed syllable of the vajra family of Vajrasattva; OM is the seed syllable of Vairochana; TRAM is the seed syllable of Ratnasambhava; HRI is the seed syllable of Amitabha; and AH is the seed syllable of Akshobya.

246. Skt. samayasattva; Tib. dam tshig sems pa. Skt. jnanasattva; Tib. ye shes sems pa.

247. All purelands dissolve into the immeasurable palace of Vajrasattva, which dissolves into the retinue, such as Bodhisattvas and Dharmapalas. Then these dissolve into the yum, or female consort, and the yum dissolves into the yab, or male consort. The yab dissolves into the vajra in his heart, the vajra dissolves into the Hundred-Syllable Mantra, and the Hundred-Syllable Mantra dissolves into the syllable HUNG in the center. The syllable HUNG dissolves from below into the nada above. [See note 9 below on the nada.]

Then one stays there, as in stainless sky, as much as one can. If the mind starts to move from habit, immediately visualize. In general, if one is visualizing oneself as Vajrasattva, it is the samayasattva, but the samayasattva is already inseparable from the jnanasattva.

248. *Nada* in a relative sense means the subtle tip of the bindu, but there is also the explanation such as the one below, in note 266 for chap. 11, which is beyond that. In *A Cascading Waterfall of Nectar*, Kyabje Thinley Norbu Rinpoche writes: "The nada is the final sign of becoming subtler and subtler before disappearing in stainless Dharmakaya. . . ." See page 155 of the paperback edition (2009).

249. Dharmakaya.

250. Visualization and dissolution come before the dedication of merit in many tantric teachings and all sadhanas of deities. This visualization and dissolution is called *du dang* in Tibetan. *Du* is dissolving into Dharmakaya. In order not to remain in the misinterpretation of eternalism's point of view of permanent gods and the existence of substantial reality, phenomena dissolve in stainless, immaterial, nonsubstantial, inconceivable Dharmakaya. *Dang* is re-arising as Rupakaya. Visualization is done in order not to remain in the misinterpretation of the nothingness of nihilist habit. Since mind is unobstructed, the unobstructed qualities of mind are transformed into the phenomena of deities. In order not to misinterpret Dharmakaya as nihilist nothingness habit, again Rupakaya arises as Vajrasattva's form and pureland. Dharmakaya emptiness and Rupakaya form show the supreme, fully enlightened state beyond the two extremes.

251. Gyurme Choying Dorje ('gyur med chos dbyings rdo rje).

252. ming byang or ming gi byang bu.

8. The Rain of Blessings

253. The Fifteenth Karmapa, Khakhyab Dorje (*mkha' khyab rdo rje*, 1871–1922).

254. The qualities of the eight branches are being pristine, cool, undisturbed, light, soft, delicious, not irritating to the throat, and soothing to the stomach.

255. o rgyan rdo rje 'chang.

256. The five lights are stainless blue, white, yellow, green, and red lights, symbolic of the five Buddha families, the origin of the wisdom form of all immeasurable Buddhas.

257. The Three Roots are the Guru, Deva, and Dakini in Sanskrit, or Lama, Yidam, and Khandro in Tibetan (bla ma, yi dam, and mkha' 'gro).

258. The five defilements are the defilements of life (as in the short life span

of sentient beings in the degenerate age), the passions, time, sentient beings, and point of view.

259. The three syllables are the white OM, red AH, and blue HUNG.

II. The Guru Yoga of Receiving Wish-Fulfilling Great Flawless Exaltation

260. Indestructible Wisdom Heruka, drinking the blood of samsaric suffering as a sign of liberating sentient beings from negative karma.

261. The vajra in his right hand and the kilaya in his left hand.

262. The curved knife is in her right hand and the kapala (skull cup) is in her left hand.

263. The recognition that one's own mind is not different from the Lama is prostration.

264. Within the land of Sambhogakaya, all flawless phenomena simultaneously, continuously, tangibly and intangibly exist, so they are the unsought self-offering.

265. In this case, the basis is not alaya, or kunzhi (kun gzhi), which is the basis of samsaric phenomena such as the phenomena of the six realms. The basis is the original purity of Dharmakaya, so the phenomena of the basis is the pure Rupakaya of immeasurable Sambhogakaya, such as the immeasurable five Buddha families and purelands, and also of Nirmakayana's land, emanated from Sambhogakaya. This is the Dzogpa Chenpo teaching on 'khor 'das kyi rnam bzhag.

266. This is nada, which cannot even be imagined. It is connected to wisdom air inseparable with stainless sky.

267. yan lag bdun pa.

About the Authors and Texts

The authors of the following Praises are unknown:

· *Praise to Jigme Lingpa (rig 'dzin 'jigs med gling pa la bstod pa)*
· *Praise to Longchenpa (kun mkhyen klong chen rab 'byams la bstod pa)*
· *Praise to Mipham Rinpoche (mi pham rin po che la bstod pa)*

KUNKHYEN LONGCHENPA (kun mkhyen klong chen pa, 1308–1364), the incomparable teacher of the Nyingma lineage, compiled and explained all the teachings and practices of the Nyingma school, composing over 250 volumes of his own writing.

· *Praise to the Melodious Wisdom Goddess Saraswati, Called "The Melody of the Youthful Display of Joy" (dbyang can ma la bstod pa gzhon nu rol dga'i dbyangs)*
· *Always Rejoicing in the Forest (Tib. nags tshal kun tu dga' ba'i gtam; Skt. Sana Ananda Pati)* is a metaphorical poetic work in which the author expresses the wish to escape the worldliness of samsara and seek refuge in the forest as a symbol for the Guru and the Triple Gems.

PATRUL RINPOCHE (dpal sprul rin po che, 1808–1887), a great Master with a nonsectarian approach, was known for the simplicity and direct style of his writing, using the common people's language. One of his major works in English translation is *The Words of My Perfect Teacher*.

· *The Practice of the View, Meditation, and Action, Called "The Sublime Heart Jewel": The Speech Virtuous in the Beginning, Middle, and End* presents advice to practitioners on the path to enlightenment, which is all contained in the three aspects of the correct view, meditation, and action, synthesized in the practice of the Six-Syllable Mantra of Avalokiteshvara.

JAMYANG KHYENTSE WANGPO ('jam dbyangs mkhyen brtse dbang po, 1820–1892), eminent Master and one of the five kingly tertöns, is also known as the First Great Khyentse Wangpo Pema Ösal Do Ngag Lingpa (mkhyen brtse dbang po pad ma 'od bsal mdo sngags gling pa). He was the founder of the Ri-me (nonsectarian) movement in Tibet.

· *Praise to Patrul Rinpoche (dpal sprul rin po che la bstod pa)*

KYABJE DUDJOM RINPOCHE (skyab rje bdud 'joms rin po che, 1904–1987), the Second Dudjom Rinpoche—also known as Jigdral Yeshe Dorje—a celebrated saint and scholar, was the Supreme Head of the Nyingma school of Tibetan Buddhism for many years. Although he was a great tertön with many treasures to reveal, he chose to devote much of his time preserving and spreading the Nyingma teachings while in exile after the Chinese invasion of Tibet. His collected works are contained in twenty-five volumes.

· *Praise to Dudjom Lingpa (bdud 'joms gling pa la bstod pa)*. Dudjom Lingpa (1835–1904), is the previous emanation of Kyabje Dudjom Rinpoche.
· *The Sadhana of Fully Enlightened Supreme Vajrasattva, Called the Daily Practice of the Profound Path, Contained in Essence* is a concise daily practice of Vajrasattva, with an explanation of how to practice for those who have died.
· *The Assembly Palace of Great, Flawless Exaltation, Radiant Lotus Light* is a concise prayer fulfilling the unconditioned wishes of the Dakinis, with clouds of flawless great exaltation of pure phenomena. (A commentary on this root text appears in *A Cascading Waterfall of Nectar* by Thinley Norbu.)
· *Calling the Lama* is a yearning devotional prayer to one's Lama, who is inseparable from one's own awareness mind.

- *The Guru Yoga of Receiving Wish-Fulfilling Great Flawless Exaltation* is a precious Guru Yoga practice of the Root Lama as Jigdral Yeshe Dorje (Kyabje Dudjom Rinpoche himself), full of the meaning of Dzogpa Chenpo. This prayer is in Kyabje Dudjom Rinpoche's Sungbum (Collected Works), vol. Ah, p. 127.

MIPHAM RINPOCHE (1846–1912), a scholar and saint of the Old Tradition (Nyingma), was recognized as brilliant from a very young age and became accomplished in all the traditions of Tibetan Buddhism. His extraordinary treatises, commentaries, and practices fill thirty-two volumes. He is known also as Chog-le Namgyal (phyogs las rnam rgyal, Victorious One of All Directions), an emanation of Manjushri.

- *Praise to Manjushri ('jam dpal la bstod pa)*
- *The Treasure of Blessings of the Ritual of Buddha* is a concise and complete practice of Buddha Shakyamuni.
- *The Rain of Blessings: Guru Yoga in Connection with the Seven-Line Prayer* is a complete, concise Guru Yoga practice in connection with the Seven-Line Prayer to Guru Rinpoche.

RIGDZIN JIGME LINGPA (1729–1798), a Dzogchen Master and tertön, was the revealer of the extensive cycle of teachings known as the Longchen Nyingtig. He was renowned for writings such as *The Treasury of Precious Qualities* and *Yeshe Lama*, the guide to Dzogchen practice. He also published the compilation of Nyingma tantras called Nyingma Gyubum.

- *Praise of the Ten Deeds of Buddha* is a prayer in which the author praises Buddha Shakyamuni through describing his activities in a lyrical way.
- *Mindfulness, the Ocean of Qualities* shows that mindfulness is indispensable even for worldly activities, especially for those who are doing spiritual practice, from beginners up to Dzogchen practitioners.

· *The Lion's Roar: Cutting Through the Errors and Deviations of the One Free from Activity, Meditating on the Heart Essence* introduces mistakes that can be encountered on the path of Dzogchen practice and explains how to overcome them.